DUE DATE

JAN 1991			
JAN 21 1991			
MAY 1 5 1991			
JUN 1 4 1991			
AUG 2 1991			
NOV 0 4 1991			
DEC 1 1991			
FEB 4			
JUN 1 8			

Seizing the Moments

Seizing the Moments

Making the Most of Life's Opportunities

James W. Moore

Abingdon Press
NASHVILLE

SEIZING THE MOMENTS:
Making the Most of Life's Opportunities

This book is printed on acid-free paper.

Library of Congress Cataloging-in-Publication Data

MOORE, JAMES W. (James Wendell), 1938–
Seizing the moments.
1. Christian life—Methodist authors.
2. Conduct of life. I. Title.

BV4501.2.M5815   1988   248.4   87-17522

ISBN 0-687-37152-X *(alk. paper)*

Scripture quotations noted KJV are from the King James Version of the Bible.

All other referenced quotations are from the Revised Standard Version of the Bible. Copyrighted 1946, 1952, © 1971, 1973 by the Division of Christian Education of the National Council of the Churches of Christ in the U.S.A. and are used by permission.

Many Scripture quotations are the author's own version.

Material on pp. 30-31 from *Living, Loving and Learning* by Leo Buscaglia (Thorofare, N.J: Charles B. Slack Inc., 1982) is used with the permission of its author.

On pp. 67-69, quotations from John Powell's *Unconditional Love,* © 1978, Tabor Publishing, Valencia, California, are used by permission of the publisher.

"My Rules" (p. 105-6) and "I'm Making a List" (p. 108) are from *Where the Sidewalk Ends* by Shel Silverstein, Copyright © 1974 by Evil Eye Music, Inc. Reprinted by permission of Harper & Row, Publishers, Inc. and Jonathan Cape Ltd., London.

On pp. 109-10, D. L. Stewart's column, which appeared originally in the *Dayton Journal Herald* and subsequently in various newspapers through the McNaught Syndicate, is used by permission of its author.

Excerpts on pp. 131-32 from *Children's Letters to God* (New York: Simon & Shuster Inc., 1975), copyright © 1975 by Eric Marshall and Stuart Hample, are reprinted by permission of Sterling Lord Literistic, Inc.

MANUFACTURED BY THE PARTHENON PRESS
NASHVILLE, TENNESSEE, UNITED STATES OF AMERICA

For my family at home,
my family at church, and
for special friends
who continue to challenge and inspire me
to seize the moments

Contents

The Tragedy of the Unseized Moment

I n the hit Broadway musical *Stop the World, I Want to Get off!* actor Anthony Newley played a kind of "everyman" character and he sang that powerful song "Once in a Lifetime." It contains these poignant words:

This is my moment . . . I'm gonna do great things.

"This is my moment." We all have known that feeling, haven't we?—that special occasion when something stirs within us and we know that a unique opportunity is now available to us, maybe never to return again in just that way. We know the feeling of the crucial moment.

Sadly, however, we must confess that we also know the empty feeling of "missing our moment," letting the moment pass. The truth is that life is a series of crucial moments, destiny moments, moments of decision. All of us have had the experience of sensing that this time, this occasion, is a special moment and we should say or do or be something. But because of fear, or timidity, or insecurity, we let the moment slip by. We do nothing, we miss our moment, and then we regret it greatly because we know deep down that we cannot reclaim it—that special moment is gone forever.

There is an interesting point here. Psychologists tell us that if we do not act every time we have this kind of feeling, we are *less* likely to act later when other such moments present themselves. Each time we fail to act, we become more closed, more hardened, more desensitized, more emotionally paralyzed.

9

A colorful illustration is found in Indian folklore. The Pima Indians believed that a stone with spikes sticking out of it was positioned next to the heart. If a person hurt or neglected someone, or did something to break down a relationship, the stone would begin to turn, and it continued to turn until the situation was set right or corrected. According to this fascinating legend, although the spikes rubbed against the heart, they did not cut or puncture it; they merely rubbed and rubbed until the heart became more and more calloused. In other words, the longer one waits to correct a situation, the more calloused one becomes.

A dramatic example is the mental patient who crouches on the floor in a fetal position, not speaking or paying attention to anyone or anything—closed in, withdrawn, turned off and tuned out. What we often do is just as paralyzing. *We trick ourselves by substituting emotion for action.* We may feel something like sympathy or appreciation or a moral commitment, but then we say, "Well, that takes care of that!" and we do nothing. We trick ourselves into thinking that just because we felt the emotion, the situation has been taken care of.

Just a few weeks ago a member of our congregation was highlighted in the local newspaper for his great community work. I was so happy to see that St. Luke's member out in the community doing significant things, out there being the church in the world. I felt a warm glow, and I thought to myself, "I'm going to clip this article out of the newspaper, and write a letter of congratulations and appreciation to let this special friend know that all of us here at St. Luke's are proud of his dedicated efforts." Now, I felt that, and I meant to do it but I didn't do a thing! I never got around to it! I felt it, but I did not act on it.

You see, that's what we do. We substitute the feeling

for the action. We trick ourselves into thinking that just
because we felt it, it has been cared for, and that is tragic!
Unless we act on the feeling, unless we act at the crucial
moment, it will soon pass, and nothing will have been
done.

- How many letters never have been written?
- How many phone calls never have been made?
- How many compliments have been left unsaid?
- How many "I'm sorrys" remain unspoken?
- How many "Thank yous" never have been said?
- How many "I love yous" are still unexpressed?
- How many commitments are still not made?—
  because we missed our moment!

If we put it off, the moment passes, the feeling subsides
and is never expressed. We see this vividly in the
Scriptures. For example, look at the rich young ruler in
Luke 18:18-24. He comes to Jesus in search of life, but
then when Jesus says, "Sell all that you have and
distribute it to the poor . . . and come, follow me" (vs.
22*b*), the young man backs off. He is inspired by Jesus.
Something stirs within him. He knows Jesus is right, that
Jesus has the answers to life. He knows deep down that he
should act; he feels it—but he turns away sorrowfully. He
has it all—wealth, youth, power—the big three! Aren't
those the things our world tells us we need to be
happy—wealth, youth, power? But look! Despite all he
has, something is missing! There is an emptiness, a void, a
vacuum, a hunger, and he sees the answer in Jesus. But
when Jesus offers him life, he turns away! He misses his
moment! He was a good man (the story makes that clear),
but he let this unique opportunity slip through his
fingers. But he is not alone. In fact, most tragic characters
of the New Testament were people who missed their
moment. Remember some of them:

- *The Elder Brother*—He missed the celebration. His pride and resentment of his brother made him miss his moment.
- *The One-talent Servant*—He squandered his opportunity and missed it.
- *The Priest and the Levite*—They tiptoed by on the other side and missed their moment.
- *The Foolish Maidens*—They missed the party because they weren't prepared to respond at the right moment.
- *Pontius Pilate*—He held in his hands the life of Jesus. He could have done great things, but he missed his moment.
- *What About Judas?*—He walked with Jesus, talked with him, ate with him, heard him teach, saw him do mighty works, felt his love. Yet the tragedy of Judas' life is that he missed his moment.

All these people graphically depict the tragedy of the unseized moment. And it is still happening. Unseized moments still come back to haunt us and fill us with regret.

Some years ago when I was a sophomore in college, a new student transferred into our school. In one classroom our chairs were in a semicircle, and he sat right across from me. Often I would look across and see him sitting there. He had the saddest face. He seemed lonely, and understandably so. He had arrived at mid-semester, didn't seem to know anyone and was always alone. I remember feeling sorry for him and thinking I ought to make an effort to welcome him, get to know him, introduce him around, befriend him. But somehow I just never got around to it.

Then one morning I picked up a paper and was shocked to read the headline: Local College Student Commits

Suicide. It was the transfer student! He had left a note saying he couldn't go on because he felt so lonely. It was then that I realized I had missed my moment of caring. In my own way, I (like the priest and the Levite) had "passed by on the other side." I (like the one-talent servant) had squandered my opportunity. I (like Pontius Pilate) had "washed my hands." I (like Judas) had missed my moment! Ronnie Gaylord's song says it well: "If there's any kindness I can show, Let me show it now." How tragic it is when we miss our moments!

It is my hope and prayer that the thoughts in this book will, through the miracle of God's grace, make us more aware, more courageous, more willing to "seize the moments"!

1

The Light-bulb Moments

Mark 1:14-15 Now after John was arrested, Jesus came into Galilee, preaching the gospel of God, and saying, "The time is ful- filled, and the kingdom of God is at hand; repent, and believe in the gospel."

L et me ask a question: How long has it been since you had a kairos moment in a chronos world? Of course, we need to begin by defining some terms. The Greek language, the original language of the New Testament, uses two different words for *time—chronos* and *kairos*.

CHRONOS TIME. The word *chronos* gives us the word *chronology*. Chronos time is drudgery time, time measured by the ticking of the clock. Each second is exactly like the one that went before it. Let me sketch in your minds the picture of chronos time.

- Picture a convict in his prison cell, checking off dates on a calendar—that's chronos time.
- Picture a man with insomnia. Unable to sleep, all he can hear is the relentless ticking of the clock pounding in his ears—that's chronos time.
- Picture an office worker who hates her job, wishing five o'clock would come so she can get get out of there—that's chronos time.
- Or picture a student sitting in a classroom, bored to tears, wanting the bell to hurry up and ring.

15

- Picture a man caught in a traffic jam, looking frantically at his watch, knowing he will be late for work, and knowing, too, that the time clock will tell on him—that's chronos time.

Chronos time is empty, meaningless, humdrum time, a void that must be filled. It is time we must put in, pass, endure, or wish away. When we talk about killing time, we are talking about chronos time.

KAIROS TIME. Kairos time represents those rich, extra-special, significant, dramatic moments that are packed with meaning, moments that stand out and stay with you for a lifetime. Kairos time is *full* time, *vital* time, *crucial* time, *decisive* time, *God's* time—those rich special moments that break into the humdrum and change your life; those powerful dramatic moments when things seem to fall into place; a new perspective comes, and God seems to be speaking to you loud and clear. That is *kairos!* Theologians would call it the moment of revelation.

Now, *kairos* is a key word in the New Testament. When Jesus came preaching, he said, "The time is fulfilled!" And the word was *kairos*, not *chronos*. It was special time, dramatic time, meaningful time. Jesus' life was packed with kairos moments. But what about yours? How long has it been since you experienced a kairos moment?

In Thornton Wilder's *Our Town*, Emily, a young woman who has died, is permitted to return to her home to relive one day with her family. She chose the day of her twelfth birthday. But when she comes back, she is very disappointed. Everyone is just too busy! Her brothers and sisters, even her father and mother, are too preoccupied with the busyness of life to stop and see the others, or even to enjoy life itself. Emily pleads with them to look at her, to see one another, to see what life is all about. But they are too busy to stop. They don't have kairos moments. They are insulated, imprisoned in their empty, harried, chronos world. Finally Emily cries out in despair, "Do any human beings ever realize life while they live it?"

How is it with you? Do you realize life while you live it? Do you have kairos moments? Or is life passing you by? The kairos moments are those significant ah-ha! experiences when the light bulb turns on, life takes on meaning, and God speaks to us loud and clear.

Let me suggest some kairos moments I know about. You will probably think of others.

The Kairos Moment of a New Insight

It's the excitement of a new understanding, a new discovery, the thrill of a new idea! There is nothing more fascinating than a new thought. Yet, so often we close our minds and give in to boredom. Let me illustrate.

One day Lucy was chasing Charlie Brown, shouting, "I'll get you, Charlie Brown. I'll catch you, and when I do, I'm going to knock your block off!"

Suddenly Charlie Brown screeched to a halt. He turned around and said, "Wait a minute, Lucy. If you and I, as relatively small children with relatively small problems, can't sit down and talk through our problems in a mature way, how can we expect the nations of the world to—"

Then POW! Lucy slugged him. She said, "I had to hit him quick. He was beginning to make sense!"

That is exactly what they did to Jesus! They "hit him quick" with a cross, because he was beginning to make sense! In my opinion, nothing was more responsible for nailing Jesus to a cross than the sin of the closed mind. The people were afraid of the kairos moment, terrified by

Jesus' new ideas, afraid of his new insights. They didn't want their dull, routine, chronos world disturbed, so they tried to silence him. Isn't that tragic?

I am haunted by a fascinating legend about some travelers crossing the desert in a camel caravan. They came to an oasis which had a strange sign: "Pick up some pebbles and put them in your pockets. Travel a day's journey, then look at the pebbles, and you will be both glad and sad!" Intrigued by the sign, the travelers obeyed. The next evening after they had traveled a day's journey, they remembered the sign. They took out the pebbles and looked at them, only to discover they had turned into gold nuggets! The sign was right. They were both glad and sad—glad they had picked up a few pebbles, but sad that they hadn't picked up a whole lot more!

Learning is like that. When I come to the end of my life, I think I will probably be both glad and sad—glad that I picked up a few nuggets of wisdom along the way, but sad that I didn't make the sacrifice to pick up a whole lot more.

So when it comes to special kairos moments, first is the moment of new insight, new learning; the excitement of a new discovery, the thrill of a new idea.

The Kairos Moment of Penitence

This is the moment that jolts the conscience and bares the soul; the penetrating moment that convicts us and reminds us that we need a Savior.

I'm thinking of King David in the Old Testament. After David had sinned with Bathsheba, the prophet Nathan told him a parable about a rich man who had many flocks and herds, but had slaughtered a poor man's only lamb.

King David was furious. "That rich man deserves to die!"

And Nathan said, "You, O king, are the man!" It was a kairos moment for David, and he repented.

I'm thinking of Alfred Nobel, the noted Swedish chemist who invented dynamite. A strange thing happened when his brother died. The newspaper somehow became confused and published the wrong obituary—that of Alfred, rather than that of the deceased brother. When Alfred Nobel read his own obituary, he was overwhelmed with guilt. The story related that he had created a substance for war, a substance that had caused much death and injury and devastation. Alfred Nobel was so convicted by that moment that he set up a foundation for an award we know as the Nobel *Peace* Prize!

A couple of weeks ago I had a kairos moment of penitence. It had been one of those days—hectic, frantic, with one emergency after another all morning long and into the afternoon. Ten minutes before an important meeting, I was driving down the street when I suddenly felt weak. I realized that I had been so busy I had missed both breakfast and lunch, so I decided to stop and pick up a quick sandwich.

I went into a small carry-out establishment and ran into the slowest sandwich-maker west of the Mississippi. I ordered a turkey sandwich and a sweet little lady started to create it. She would pick up a piece of bread and smile at me and nod. I would smile and nod back. Then she would begin to spread the mayonnaise. She worked with that sandwich so slowly I began to pace. I cleared my throat nervously and looked at my watch impatiently, but to no avail. She would not hurry.

Finally my patience wore thin. I decided I simply couldn't wait any longer, so I raised my hand to wave to her to just forget the sandwich.

At that moment, she looked at me. "Sir, may I ask you a question? Don't you work at St. Luke's Methodist Church?"

"Yes, ma'am," I answered.

"You're Jim Moore, aren't you? The minister at St. Luke's?"

"Yes, ma'am."

"I can't believe this," she said. "My husband will be so thrilled to know you were here. You see, we watch your service on television every Sunday, and we just love your church. Your choir is wonderful, and we even like your sermons. My husband had a stroke about a year ago, and the highlight of his week is Sunday morning when your church service comes on. Would you sign this napkin so I can show him that you came in?" Then she added, "By the way, were you about to say something?"

I replied, "I was just about to say that you certainly do make a fine sandwich!"

I walked out of that shop with a turkey sandwich in my hand and a prayer of penitence in my heart: "O God, forgive me; help me to be understanding. Teach me to always be kind; deliver me from impatience."

The Kairos Moment of a Tender Love Experience

The moment touches us deeply. It is that special moment when love feels so right, when two people, for a brief moment, become the whole world for each other.

One Sunday morning several years ago, I had a kairos moment like that. We had just finished the worship service, and I was standing at the Communion rail, greeting people. It was a hectic scene, and my mind was darting in all directions. People were speaking; I was trying to make some new members feel welcome; someone was telling me about a friend in the hospital; another was introducing a visitor; everything was confused.

Suddenly I felt a tug on my robe. I turned and looked

down. It was our son, Jeff, five years old at the time, standing there with a small tomato plant growing out of some black dirt in a styrofoam cup. He was motioning for me to bend down. My first reaction was typically parental—to say, "Not now, Jeff, there's too much going on. Couldn't this wait till we get in the car?" Instead, I dropped to one knee beside him.

And he said, "Dad, I've been growing this tomato plant in Sunday school. We've been learning how God makes things grow. It's really mine, but I want you and Momma to have it. You are always doing things for me and giving me things, and now I want to give this tomato plant to you because I love you so much!"

That was a kairos moment. Nothing else in the world mattered, and for that brief moment as we hugged tightly, we became the whole world for each other.

Jesus' life and ministry were packed with kairos moments like that. He could walk into a busy street scene and see a Zacchaeus, hear the cries of a blind Bartimaeus, feel the touch of a sick woman at the hem of his garment. Be honest. How long has it been since you felt moved by the touch of tender, genuine love? How long has it been since you had a kairos moment of love in this chronos world?

The Kairos Moment of Inspiration

You are moved to action in this moment of inspiration when God touches you and calls you to a special job.

Moses at the burning bush sensed the presence of God, the call of God; it was a moment of inspiration and God put him to work, moved him to action. "Go, Moses, and set my people free! Go and I will go with you!" And Moses went, because it was a kairos moment of inspiration.

How long has it been since you were inspired—

inspired in a way that makes you feel you can't sit still, that you must respond, that you must act upon it, that you must do something about it? How long has it been since you were spiritually moved?

God is calling people right now to special tasks and special commitments. Some will respond. But sadly, many will not, because so many of us have grown so accustomed to our routine, uneventful chronos world that we insulate ourselves. We hold God at arm's length and thus will not permit the kairos moment of inspiration to penetrate our lives.

According to the legend of the touchstone, if you could find the stone on the coast of the Black Sea and hold it in your hand, everything you touched would turn to gold. You could recognize the touchstone by its warmth. The other stones would feel cold, but the touchstone would turn warm in your hand.

Once a man sold everything he had, went to the Black Sea, and began picking up stones, hoping to find the touchstone. After some days had passed, he realized he was picking up the same stones again and again. So he devised a plan: Pick up a stone; if it's cold, throw it into the sea. This he did for weeks and weeks. One morning he picked up a stone that felt cold, and he threw it into the sea. He picked up another that felt cold, and he threw it into the sea. He picked up yet another stone. It turned warm in his hand, and before he realized what he was doing, he had thrown it into the sea! This can happen to us. We can come upon a kairos moment and be so dulled by routine that, before we realize it, we throw it away.

Life is packed with kairos moments. My prayer is that we won't miss them; that we will be warmed by them and keep holding them and celebrate them, not toss them into the sea. My prayer is that we will seize those moments!

2

The Moments of Opportunity

Matthew 25:14-18 "For it will be as when a man going on a journey called his servants and entrusted to them his property; to one he gave five talents, to another two, to another one, to each according to his ability. Then he went away. He who had received the five talents went at once and traded with them; and he made five talents more. So also, he who had the two talents made two talents more. But he who had received the one talent went and dug in the ground and hid his master's money.

Let me begin with three quick stories. Note, if you will, the common thread that runs through them.

The first story comes from the great British minister Leslie Weatherhead. When Dr. Weatherhead was a young man working his way through college, he took a job one summer as a door-to-door salesman. He had many memorable experiences that summer, but the incident he remembered most vividly was one that saddened him greatly: The family that met him at the door had said coldly, "Son, you are wasting your time here, 'cause we ain't interested in nothing!"

The second story is from the pen of noted Austrian novelist Franz Kafka. In one of his novels, Kafka tells a parable about a man who waited all his life outside a door. He looked at the door wistfully and longed to enter. He watched the door keeper and wondered how to get past him and through the door. He plotted and strategized, schemed and planned, but was afraid to try. Finally he gave up, tired, disappointed, and disillusioned.

As the man was dying, he said to the doorkeeper, "Why? Why did you keep me out?"

"I didn't," answered the doorkeeper. "This is your door and I am here to serve you."

"Then why did you stand in my way?"

"I didn't," replied the doorman. "I would have been more than glad to open the door for you, but you never asked to come in!"

The third story is based on history. Some years ago in South America, a crew of Peruvian sailors, cruising up the Amazon River, came upon a strange sight. It was like a scene from "The Twilight Zone." A Spanish ship was at anchor in the middle of the wide Amazon River, and all the sailors were stretched out weakly on the deck of the ship. As the Peruvians drew closer, they saw that the Spaniards were in terrible physical condition. They looked the picture of death itself, their lips parched and swollen. They were literally dying of thirst.

"Can we help you?" shouted the Peruvians.

The Spaniards cried out, "Water! Water! We need fresh water!"

The Peruvian sailors, surprised at this request, told them to lower their buckets and help themselves.

The Spanish mariners had thought they were lost in the open ocean, that the water around them was undrinkable. So they had given up hope. They had quit trying. They just dropped anchor and waited to die of thirst. Only a couple of miles up the Amazon River, they had been anchored in the midst of fresh water for days and didn't know it. They had not discovered it because they had quit trying.

Now, of course, the thread that runs through these stories is the problem of apathy. *Apathy* means quitting on life. It is the opposite of faith. It is the opposite of hope. It is opposite of love. It is the opposite of commitment. To be *apathetic*, according to *Roget's International Thesaurus*, is to be *spiritless, heartless, sluggish*. It is to be *numb, paralyzed, insensitive*. To be apathetic is to be *unconcerned, unimpressed, unexcited, unmoved, unstirred, untouched*.

I saw a bumper sticker the other day with this message: "If I were concerned about anything, I would really be upset about apathy."

We all dread the thought of failure, but worse than trying and failing is not trying at all. Apathy is not trying at all, and it is the worst failure of all. If you try and fail, at least you know you are alive, still in the game. But not trying at all means you have quit on life, you are numbered among the "walking dead."

The silent tragedy of life is that many people reach the point of death only to find they have never really *lived*, never really *loved*, never really *tried*. Somewhere along the way (often quite early) they were hurt or scared or disappointed, and they quit. They refused to try anymore. Terrified by the risks and pressures and demands of life, afraid of commitment, they pulled back into their shells and hid.

Jesus once told a parable about this kind of quiet tragedy. We call it the parable of the talents. A more contemporary name might be the parable of the investments. Like all his parables, it is simple, yet profound in its implications.

The businessman who decided to take a trip had left his fortune with three men. When he returned from his travels, he called in his associates for a report. The first two men who had invested their money were commended for a job well done. But the third man, who had been afraid, not only missed out on a promotion but lost all the money and his position as well.

Apathy is costly. Jesus shows us that in this parable, and he also exposes the perfect formula for failure! Let me show you how that could be outlined.

The third servant failed for three reasons: First, he didn't appreciate what he had; second, he didn't accept what he had; third, he didn't use what he had. Let's look at these three ideas.

He Didn't Appreciate What He Had.

Can't you just hear him complaining, "I didn't get as much as the others. It's not fair! How can I hope to compete with them? It's not right, so I won't play the game. I'll show 'em. I won't participate at all!" Here we have bitterness and apathy and ingratitude.

He had received a talent, worth 6,000 silver coins, but he didn't appreciate it. In fact, he may well have resented it, because in his mind it paled in comparison to the money the others had received. One of our big problems is lack of appreciation.

A few summers ago we went with our youth choir to England. We stayed in the homes of English people, and we noticed that many of them, though they lived in a frugal way, seemed so grateful for what they had. It made me ashamed that we so often take for granted the many, many things we have. This ungrateful attitude is dangerous because ingratitude leads to apathy, and apathy, as we have seen, is the worst failure of all.

I once heard a wonderful story about a farmer who had lived on the same farm all his life, but now he desperately craved a change. So he decided to sell the old place and buy another more to his liking. He listed the farm with a real estate agent, who looked over the property and prepared an ad for the newspaper.

The agent read to the farmer this very flattering description: "Beautiful farmhouse, ideal location, excellent barn, good pasture, fertile soil, up-to-date equipment, well-bred stock. Near town, near church, near school. Good neighbors."

"Wait a minute," said the farmer. "Read that again."

And again the description was read: "Beautiful farmhouse, ideal location . . . "

"Changed my mind," said the farmer. "I'm not gonna sell. All my life I've been looking for a place just like that!"

Can't we relate to that? That farmer was living in a paradise and didn't know it. Dr. Russell Conwell's great lecture "Acres of Diamonds," which he gave more than six thousand times, was built around this idea that the riches of life are all around us, but so often our eyes fail to see them. We magnify the difficulties, overlook the advantages, and fail to see the good in what we have. The servant in Jesus' parable had this problem, and too often, so do we.

He Didn't Accept What He Had.

Jesus' parable reminds us that we can't always determine the size of our talents—that is, there are certain givens in life. Some things cannot be changed. We must learn to live with some things that cannot be altered. All the bitterness in the world would not change the fact that the man received one talent. That's what he was given, that's what he had to work with. No matter how much energy we expend, it is just a fact that there are some things in life—in your life and mine—that will not change. Life has limits we must learn to accept.

One writer has suggested that this is partly what the

Adam and Eve story is about. God had placed them in the garden and given them incredible possibilities. They could name the animals and subdue them, they could till the earth, they could enjoy all the wonderful works of nature, they could feast on the fruit of the land. Indeed, Adam and Eve could do everything *except* one thing.

They had *one limitation!* They were not to eat of the fruit of one tree in the midst of the garden. It's almost as if this is a reminder that we are not God; we have some limits on our lives. There are some things we cannot do and some things we cannot change! We all must come to terms with the "trees" in our lives:

- Those of us 5'11" tall cannot be 6'5".
- Most of us never will run the four-minute mile or become Miss America.
- Most of us never will be famous or beautiful or ingenious.
- We cannot control gravity.
- We cannot call back cruel words already spoken.
- We cannot change our past.
- We cannot change the aging process, and we cannot eliminate death.

I could go on and on, pointing out numerous things in our lives that cannot be changed. The real question is this: How do we respond to these "trees" in the midst of our garden?

Some people spend their lives running away from them. That's what the one-talent servant did. He tried to run away. He hid the money to escape the pressure.

Some people go through life playing the "if only" game: If only I were taller, or smarter; if only I had married someone else, or had never married at all; if only I had gone to a different college, or had that house or that car; if only I had been born rich, or had more than six thousand silver coins. The "if only" game doesn't work. Those who play it fail to face reality; resenting their limitations they become bitter, cynical, and miserable.

The Christian answer is *serenity of acceptance*, even the redemption of our handicaps. This is what Jesus was doing in the Garden of Gethsemane: "Father, I don't want this cup, but if I must, I will drink it. Thy will be done!" That is "serenity of acceptance."

The last servant had less than the other two, but he had enough. He had enough to do something good, meaningful, creative, productive. But because he would not accept what he had, he did *nothing*. I wonder how often that happens to us.

He failed first because he didn't *appreciate* what he had. He failed because he didn't *accept* what he had.

Now there is another thought to consider:

He Didn't Use What He Had.

I have a friend I wish you could meet. His name is Bret, and he was born unusually short. That is a "given" in his life. He is twenty years old now, and if he were to stand beside me, he would not come to my waist. He is a junior at Louisiana Tech University.

I'll never forget the first time I saw him. He was eight years old, a third-grader at Riverside Elementary School. He was running in some races during a field day, and I was impressed by his spunk and spirit. His legs were so short he didn't have a chance to win; he ran in three races that day, and in every one, he finished last. But his mother, waiting at the finish line, would run and hug him and say, "Bret, you ran really well. I'm so proud of you!"

Bret did not win a single ribbon, but if I had had some gold medals, I would have put one on Bret, and another on his mother. Bret captured the hearts of everyone there that day because though he didn't have much chance to win, he did his best. He used what he had.

On that same day, there was another little boy the same age, sitting under a tree and pouting because he remembered that the year before he hadn't won a blue ribbon. So this year he decided that rather than risk not winning, he just wouldn't run at all. Rather than risk failure, he wouldn't even try.

The teachers pleaded with him, his mother pleaded with him, the other students pleaded with him, but he just sat there all day and never got in the game at all.

Bret didn't win a blue ribbon, but he was a winner that day, and he still is. He's in college, drives a car, has a job, and smiles at everyone he meets. And everyone he meets loves him because he uses what he has.

We often put off using what we have. Leo Buscaglia, a professor in Southern California, often assigned a paper in which students responded to the question: "If you had only five days to live, how would you spend those five days? And with whom?" The responses are interesting. Some students indicated they would say "I'm sorry" or "I love you." Some wrote that they would "walk on the beach and watch a sunrise." They turned in their papers, and when they got them back, written on them was a note: "Why don't you do these things *now?*"

I have often wondered whether the one-talent servant might have been trying to get up the nerve to do something, but his employer came back before he was ready. Procrastination—what a problem that is for us! Leo Buscaglia speaks of this, too, in *Living, Loving and Learning:*

There was a girl who gave me a poem, and she gave me permission to share it with you, and I want to do that because it explains about putting off and putting off and putting off—especially putting off caring about people we really love. She wants to remain anonymous, but she calls the poem, "Things You Didn't Do." And she says this:

Remember the day I borrowed your brand new car and I dented it?
I thought you'd kill me, but you didn't.
And remember the time I dragged you to the beach, and you said it would rain, and it did?
I thought you'd say, "I told you so." But you didn't.
Do you remember the time I flirted with all the guys to make you jealous, and you were?
I thought you'd leave me, but you didn't.
Do you remember the time I spilled strawberry pie all over your car rug?
I thought you'd hit me, but you didn't.
And remember the time I forgot to tell you the dance was formal and you showed up in jeans?
I thought you'd drop me, but you didn't.
Yes, there were lots of things you didn't do.
But you put up with me, and you loved me, and you protected me.
There were lots of things I wanted to make up to you when you returned from Viet Nam.
But you didn't.

The point is clear. Don't wait. Do it now. If you have a word of love that needs to be expressed, say it now. If you have a broken relationship that ought to be mended, don't let the sun go down tonight without setting it right. If you have something you need to be doing, seize the moment! Do it now!

The one-talent servant is the picture of apathy. He didn't appreciate what he had, he didn't accept what he had, and he didn't use what he had. That is the perfect formula for failure!

3

The Moments of Grief

Psalm 23 The Lord is my shepherd, I shall not want;
he makes me lie down in green pastures.
He leads me beside still waters;
he restores my soul.
He leads me in paths
of righteousness
for his name's sake.

Even though I walk through the valley of the shadow of death,
I fear no evil;
for thou art with me;

thy rod and thy staff,
they comfort me.

Thou preparest a table before me
in the presence of my enemies;
thou anointest my head with oil,
my cup overflows.

Surely goodness and mercy shall follow me
all the days of my life;
and I shall dwell in the house of the LORD
forever.

When our hearts are broken, when we must walk through the grief valley, how does God bring healing?

I don't want to be morbid or sensational or overly emotional, but I would like to be very personal. I am thinking about my own recent experience with sorrow—the sudden loss of my mother in an automobile accident in Winston-Salem, North Carolina, on December 17—the week before Christmas.

Grief is a painful experience. It hurts! It is an intense feeling of loss, an agonizing experience of separation from someone we love very much. Grief is the by-product of love, and as "cliche-ish" as it may sound, it is still profoundly true: It is better to have loved and lost than never to have loved at all.

But there is much more to learn from the grief experience. In these recent days of personal mourning, I have had old ideas reaffirmed and verified, and I'm learning new things. Sorrow has much to teach us. Remember how Robert Browning Hamilton put it in "Along the Road":

> I walked a mile with Pleasure
> She chattered all the way
> But left me none the wiser
> For all she had to say.

> I walked a mile with Sorrow,
> And ne'er a word said she;
> But, oh, the things I learned from her
> When Sorrow walked with me.

It was a Monday morning. I had been sick with a virus and my temperature had been high most of the night, but I was determined to get up and make it to work. The temperature was normal now, but I was so weak I could hardly hold my head up as I tried to get ready. We had an important staff meeting scheduled that morning and I felt I really needed to be there. My wife kept looking at me with that "I can't believe you are trying to go to work" look that only a wife can write across her face.

Finally I realized she was right. I could not make it. I was too weak. My head was pounding and I was still aching. Reluctantly, I crawled back into bed. I thought to myself as I settled in that, during twenty years in the ministry, this was the first day I would miss because of sickness. I also remember thinking, I'm over the hill. This is what happens when you are forty. After forty, it's all maintenance!

Just about then the phone rang. It was answered in the kitchen. I couldn't hear what was said, but I could tell something was wrong. Alarm, urgency, bad vibrations were in the air. I started to get up. My wife ran down the hallway and into the bedroom. Then, through tears, she said words that seared into my memory: "Jim, it's your sister, Susie, calling from Winston-Salem. Your mother was killed in a car wreck this morning!"

I grabbed for the phone. My mind raced. This can't be! We had lost our father in the same way some years before. This must be a bad dream. I'll wake up in a minute. It's unbelievable! Too sudden—too fast—too final! But no matter how my mind protested, it was true. It had happened. One so vibrant, so alive, so thoughtful, so loving—suddenly gone.

Quickly, numb with shock, we mechanically set up a conference call so that Susie in North Carolina, my brother, Bob, in Memphis, and I in Shreveport could all get on the phone, find out what had happened, and make the necessary arrangements, the essential decisions.

The story unfolded. Mother's last act had been one of thoughtfulness. (I will always cherish that memory.) Her neighbor was going into downtown Winston-Salem to take her niece to an early morning bus. Mother, concerned about her friend, went along so her friend would not make the trip back home alone. The accident occurred right by the bus terminal in a twenty-mile-per-hour zone. If only they had been a little earlier or a little later. Mother was in the back seat and was the only one hurt. The doctors told us she probably died quickly, if not instantly, with severe head and chest injuries and cardiac arrest. She was a young sixty-three.

In subsequent days, we have walked through the valley of sorrow. As we move through the "grief process" we feel the presence of God as never before—God has touched us in many different ways to heal where it hurts. Let me tell you some of the ways God brings healing to a broken heart, as we are experiencing it.

God Heals Through the Use of Time.

Time heals! It's true—it does! God uses time to heal wounds. The loss of a loved one is a kind of emotional amputation. A real part of you is gone and it is hard to get used to that idea. We have read of people, for example, who have had a leg amputated but still feel an itch in the foot that is no longer there. The brain has not adapted to the fact that the leg and foot are gone. In time, the brain adapts to the absence of the leg. But this does not occur immediately; it is a slow process; it takes time. In like manner, the emotional amputation involved in the grief process takes time.

Indeed, a key to understanding the grief process is to remember that grief is a *journey,* a pilgrimage, something we "pass through." The psalmist spoke of "going through the valley of the shadow." Jesus spoke of the strength that comes from "going through mourning." Grief is a journey, and it takes time to make the pilgrimage, because we must pass through certain stages along the way.

Let me illustrate. If I drive from Houston to Dallas on the Interstate, I must pass through Conroe, Huntsville, Madisonville, and Corsicana. Before I start, I know it is going to take time—at least four and a half hours. (The only way to get there faster by automobile is to ride with A. J. Foyt.) It takes a certain amount of time to make that trip, and there are certain places to pass through. The caution here is that we dare not stay too long at any one place. If you stop in Conroe, you'll never get to Dallas.

God heals us by taking us, in time, through these grief stages. It helps if we can call them by name. Like traveling a familiar highway, when we know that Conroe is just over the hill—and then Huntsville and Madisonville—we can anticipate the route, and it makes the journey easier. If we recognize the stages of grief, it makes the journey easier:

NUMBNESS. This feeling is a rather intriguing mixture of shock and strength—almost as if God anesthetizes us to get us through those first difficult hours and days.

THE STAGE OF EXPRESSED EMOTIONS. I went through a time when I was fine until I saw someone I love. That made my eyes well up with tears and my voice choke away to nothing. During that period we need to cry it out, work it out, talk it out, pray it out.

EXISTENTIAL LONELINESS. The relationship is unique: "No one feels it quite like I do." No one can do it for us. We must walk the valley alone . . . and yet not alone—the Father is with us. His family, his children are with us.

A PERIOD OF QUESTIONING. Why? Why did this have to happen? If only the car had been ten seconds earlier, five seconds later—scant seconds either way, and it would not have happened.

THE GUILT STAGE. Why didn't I call more often? Why didn't I visit more often? Why didn't I write more often? Why didn't I say "I love you" more often?

THE RETURN TO REALITY. Finally we gain the strength to pick up and go on with life. The mark of faith and victory is the ability to go on. And it is the finest tribute we can pay to the one whose loss we mourn.

You see, grief is a journey, a journey that takes time. And as we move through the valley, God anoints us in his own time, in his own special way, with the balm of healing.

God Heals Through the Love and Support of Others.

All my life I have heard this and I have preached it, but I never have felt it more strongly than I feel it right now.

Your love in our time of sorrow has sustained and inspired us in ways I cannot express in words. We have felt the touch of God through you. Your acts of love, your letters, flowers, telegrams, gifts, thoughtful calls, kind words, tender handshakes, gentle hugs, visits—and most of all, your prayers—have sustained us more than you will ever know. Your loving, caring touch is for us the healing touch of God.

God Brings Healing Through Family Relationships.

- Family members drawing together, helping and supporting one another.
- The children sensing the tenderness of the moment and rising to the occasion, expressing a maturity beyond their years.
- The older children, Wendell, Cissy, Jodi, and Jeff, taking care of the younger children.
- Jodi and Jeff again and again gently touching my arm, asking, "Are you okay, Dad?"
- Seven-year-old Brantley telling his mother, "I'm glad Leslie and Julie are too young to understand this, or we would have two more hurt hearts."

- My brother and his wife, Cynthia, gathering the family in their home in a love circle for prayer when we first came together.
- Little Leslie, wanting to do her part the morning of the funeral, gathering us in the den and singing every Christmas carol in the hymnal, with her own four-year-old brand of choreography to keep us "entertained." Then, like a scene from a Norman Rockwell painting, reading the Christmas story with the Bible upside down.
- Our brother-in-law, Tommy, hurting as though he had lost his own mother, because she loved him like a son.
- The family planning the funeral, wanting it to be a celebration of life, a celebration of faith, hope, and love, a remembering of her life and of God's promises.
- My brother and sister asking my co-pastor, D. L. Dykes, to conduct the funeral, because they knew that would be especially meaningful to me.

Through these kinds of family experiences, God brings healing.

God Brings Healing Through Truth-Gathering.

The hardest thing for me was the "suddenness" of it, but alongside that was the uncertainty . . . being so far away and not knowing exactly what happened—and wanting desperately to know. I don't know if this is the case with everybody, but I found myself hungry for every detail. What caused the accident? Where did it occur? How did death come? Was anyone else hurt? How quickly did the ambulance get there? What was the weather like? What were the streets like? What exactly did the doctors say?

Gathering this information seemed to help me. I don't know why. But I remember that verse of Scripture: "The truth shall set you free!"

God Heals Through the Gift of Memory.

The gift of memory is a wonderful gift from God. Every time I see a sugar cookie I will remember my mother and her love for her grandchildren. She knew how much they loved sugar cookies, and she always had a big supply on hand. I cherish that kind of memory. It reminds me of her love and thoughtfulness. I will also cherish the fact that the last three things I know of that my mother did were act of kindness:

- At the time of the accident she was trying to help a friend, being a good neighbor. She died as she lived, thinking of others.

- On the Sunday night before the accident, she was to go caroling with friends from church. Instead, she stayed behind with a sick little boy so that the boy's parents could go to the caroling party. She said, "I can't sing much anyway."

- And then, on the morning after the accident—the morning after her death—a tender moment for us . . . we received in the mail our Christmas gifts from her, thoughtfully selected, carefully wrapped, lovingly prepared.

Memories to hold on to, memories to cherish, memories through which God brings healing.

Healing Comes Through Faith.

As Dr. Dykes expressed it so magnificently in the funeral service, a worship service, when he spoke so powerfully: "God is on both sides of the grave. Death is not really death at all. Rather, it is movement from one dimension of life with God to a deeper dimension of life with God. He is the Father who loves his children and who has prepared a place for us. He is the Good Shepherd, and because of him we can walk through the valley of the shadow of death without fear, for he is with us."

In some ways it is hard to lose a loved one at Christmas. But on the other hand, the message of Christmas is our hope, our glad tidings of comfort and joy, our good news. In Matthew's Christmas story, he captures the message in one word—Emmanuel—God with us. Christ came to underscore this "good news of great joy" that God is love, and he is with us, and nothing can separate us from him. Did you hear that? *Nothing* can separate us from him—not even death!

That is our faith; that is God's promise; that is the message of Christmas—EMMANUEL—he is with us!

Let me conclude with two quick observations:

First, we need to keep up to date on our relationships. This week a close friend of mine came by and said, "Jim, I had to talk with you today to tell you how much you and your family have been in my thoughts and prayers . . . and also to tell you that the accident has jolted me dramatically. I don't know whether it's because of our close friendship or because we are about the same age or because I am so close to my mother, but your experience has touched me deeply. It has reminded me how important it is that we keep up to date."

I misunderstood him. I thought he meant keep up to date with business matters—a will, insurance policies, things like that—but no.

He said, "That's important, but not what I'm talking about. We need to keep up to date on our relationships. We never know what may happen, or how suddenly. We need to keep up to date on our relationships with our parents, with our brothers and sisters, with ourselves. We need to keep up to date on our relationships with our church . . . and with God." He is so right!

Second, we must go forward. When someone we love dies, we must go on. Like riding a bicycle, the only way to keep your balance is to go forward. If you stand still, you will topple over. When Jesus healed people, sometimes he said something like this: "Go your way. Your faith has made you whole." Let me paraphrase that: "Go on your way. Go forward. Go on with life. I will go with you . . . and as you go, your faith will make you whole!"

4

The Moments of Trust

Exodus 14:10-15 When Pharaoh drew near, the people of Israel lifted up their eyes, and behold, the Egyptians were marching after them; and they were in great fear. And the people of Israel cried out to the LORD; and they said to Moses, "Is it because there are no graves in Egypt that you have taken us away to die in the wilderness? What have you done to us, in bringing us out of Egypt? Is not this what we said to you in Egypt, 'Let us alone and let us serve the Egyptians'? For it would have been better for us to serve the Egyptians than to die in the wilderness." And Moses said to the people, "Fear not, stand firm, and see the salvation of the LORD, which he will work for you today; for the Egyptians whom you see today, you shall never see again. The LORD will fight for you, and you have only to be still." The LORD said to Moses, "Why do you cry to me? Tell the people of Israel to go forward."

Some years ago when Lou Holtz was head football coach of the Arkansas Razorbacks, he said something we all can relate to about the troubles we face in the living of these days: "I know God doesn't send us more trouble than we can handle, but sometimes I think he overestimates my ability!"

I suppose we all feel that way at times. Moses and the people of Israel must have felt that way when they were caught between the Pharaoh's powerful pursuing army and the deep Red Sea.

Moses experienced the presence of God in a burning bush and through that dramatic encounter felt called to go to Egypt to bring the people of Israel out of slavery and into freedom in the Promised Land. Remember how reluctant Moses was to take on that difficult task? He was not overjoyed with the prospect of facing the Egyptian

Pharaoh and telling him to let those people go. You could lose your head by talking like that to an Egyptian king. Moses knew it was a dreadful task. To face the Pharaoh was fearsome enough. But persuading him to go along with the idea of freeing the Israelite slaves was well-nigh impossible—and Moses knew it.

But God said, "Go Moses, and tell Pharaoh to set my people free! Go, Moses, and I will go with you!"

So Moses went forward, not sure how this was going to turn out but trusting God to be with him. Then after a series of confrontations and conferences and dialogues and debates and plagues, finally the Pharaoh gave in. He gave the Israelites their freedom. Quickly, Moses rallied them and led them out of Egypt, out of slavery.

The people of Israel were filled with joy. This was a historic moment. This was their Exodus, their deliverance, their salvation. But as they made camp at the Red Sea, they looked back. On the horizon they saw a huge cloud of dust. Listening, they heard the unmistakable rumble of chariots. They knew what that meant! Pharaoh had changed his mind. His army was coming after them. The people of Israel realized their great problem. They were trapped, pinned in, cornered, caught between the Pharaoh's army and the deep Red Sea.

Interestingly, as we read between the lines of this dramatic story in the book of Exodus, we can see several different ways people respond to trouble. Let's look at these, because they seem to be the ways people still deal with trouble today, and we just might find ourselves somewhere in the story.

If somehow we could get into a time capsule and go back to that scene beside the Red Sea, just as the Israelites realize they are in big trouble and begin to deal with their problem, we might well overhear these classic responses:

Let's Go Back Where We Were!

Let's go back to the good old days. What have you done to us, Moses? Why did you have to bring us out of Egypt? Why didn't you leave us alone and let us serve the Egyptians? Things weren't so bad back there. What we had was a lot better than being trapped out here. We never did it this way before! Let's go back!

I was in a workshop one summer at Lake Junaluska in North Carolina. The leader was the nationally known writer and consultant Lyle Schaller. One morning he put before us this fascinating question: "What is the single most powerful influence in the decision-making process? For example, If you are in a group, trying to make a decision about something, or trying to plan an event or a course of action, what is the most powerful influence in the room?"

How would you answer that? Well, we discussed it for a while, and several interesting answers emerged. But then Schaller gave us his answer. He said, "No question about it, the most powerful influence in decision making is *the past.*" He is right on target.

Think about that for a moment. If you are in a group trying to decide something, and you are having difficulty, what do you do? Well, you ask What did we do last year? And nine times out of ten, you do the same thing again.

When in doubt, what do we do? We go back. We back off! We go back to the familiar, back to the good old days, totally forgetting that the good old days had their share of problems.

Isn't that the way some people face trouble? Afraid to stand up to the challenge, they want to retreat, go back where they were.

Let's Run Away and Hide!

This ploy is as old as the Garden of Eden. As soon as
Adam and Eve had a problem, what did they do? They
tried to run away and hide. People are still trying to do
that, aren't they? People are still trying to run away from
their problems, hide behind their "escapism crutches."
But you can't really hide from trouble. The Israelites
certainly couldn't hide their thousands of people in the
desert.

During the war between the States, a Union soldier
from Ohio was shot in the arm during the battle of Shiloh.

His captain saw he was injured and barked an order:
"Gimme your gun, Private, and get to the rear!"

The private handed over his rifle and ran toward the
north, seeking safety. But after covering two or three
hundred yards, he came upon another skirmish. Then he
ran to the east and ran into another part of the battle.
Then he ran west, but encountered more fighting there.

Finally he ran back to the front lines, shouting:
"Gimme my gun back, Cap'n. There ain't no rear to this
battle!"

Precisely. When it comes to the troubles of this world,
there "ain't no rear" to the battle! You can't really run
away and hide.

Let's Feel Sorry for Ourselves!

This is the way many people choose to deal with their
problems. They just quit on life. They give in to self-pity.
They have nothing left to deal with their problems
creatively because they are expending all their energy
crying, Woe is me! and feeling sorry for themselves.

A couple of years ago, an Atlanta newspaper ran a
wonderful human interest story about a young mother

who was trying to give some liquid medicine to her two-year-old son. The child would not cooperate. He would shut his mouth tightly, shake his head from side to side, and hit at the spoon with both hands. The young mother coaxed, she pleaded, she threatened, she bribed, to no avail. He would not take his medicine! Finally, worn down, the young mother gave in to self-pity. She threw down the spoon, fled into her room, and fell across the bed, sobbing.

In a few minutes, she heard loud laughter coming from the kitchen. Curious, she went to investigate and found that Grandmother had solved the problem. She had mixed the medicine with orange juice, put it in a water pistol, and was shooting it into the wide-open mouth of the delighted little boy!!

We have only so much energy. If we use it all up in self-pity, we won't have any left for creative solutions.

Let's Find Someone to Blame!

Isn't it interesting? When something goes wrong, one of the first things we want to do is find someone to blame it on! Look at the Israelites at the Red Sea. They see that cloud of dust on the horizon being kicked up by Pharaoh's army, and immediately they turn on Moses. Moments ago he was their champion, their leader, their hero, but now when trouble rears its head, they go for the jugular. "It's all your fault, Moses! A fine mess you've gotten us into. Why did we ever listen to you? You're the one to blame for this."

Some years ago I had a poignant experience while working with an alcoholic. He had been missing for more than a month. He left home drunk on Christmas Eve and staggered back on January 31. His wife, who had left him, called and asked me to check on him.

When I knocked on the door, I heard something crash
to the floor inside. The man was stumbling around in a
drunken stupor. I knocked again and called his name. I
heard him fall to the floor and begin crawling toward the
door. He fumbled with the doorknob, and when he finally
pushed the door open he was lying face down on the floor.
He saw my feet, slowly turned his head upward, and
found himself looking into the face of his minister. I guess
at that moment, I must have looked ten feet tall.

He was dirty, covered with the filth of his own
drunkenness, and had not washed or shaved or changed
clothes for over a month. When he saw me, he began to
cry.

I helped him up and got him on the couch. I washed his
face and tried to get some food and coffee into him.
Suddenly he turned on me and began to blame me for his
problem. Then he blamed his wife, then his parents, and
then he started in on his neighbors and those "hypocrites
down at the church." He blamed the mayor, the
President, and the Congress. He even cursed God for
letting him be born.

He turned back to me. "Well, aren't you going to say
anything?"

I answered, "I was just wondering whether there's
anybody else we could think of to blame this on."

He looked at me angrily, and for a moment I thought I
had gone too far. But then he looked down, and after a few
moments of silence, he said, "It's all my fault! I've made
such a mess of my life, haven't I?"

"Well," I answered, "you are a mess right now, but
your life is not over. You can start again."

He paused for a moment. "Jim, do you really believe
that? Do you really believe God can help me whip this
thing?"

And I said, "I surely do, but the real question is, do you

believe it, and are you ready to do something about it?
Are you ready to admit you've got a problem and need
help?"

Evidently he was, because he went to A.A. And now
with their help, with his church's help, with his family's
help, and with God's help, he is whipping it. He called
me the other day. He hasn't had a drink in almost twenty
years. He knows he still has a problem. He is one drink
away from big trouble. But he also knows he can't blame
anybody else.

When we take responsibility for our own lives, our
communities will help us, our families will help us, our
church will help us, and God will help us. You see, the
truth is, we don't need scapegoats. We have a Savior!

Let's Go Forward . . . Trusting God!

Though caught between the Pharaoh and the deep Red
Sea, Moses did not give up, he did not quit, he did not
throw in the towel. No, he trusted God. Andwent
forward.

When trouble suddenly erupts, remember Moses at
the Red Sea. He didn't have all the answers, but he did
stay in communication with God. And he did go forward,
and he did do his best, and he did trust God to bring it out
right.

Some years ago when I was visiting a small church in
Memphis, I was much moved and impressed by the
prayer of the minister. He was an older man and had
evidently recently gone through some kind of trouble. I
can remember his prayer as if I had heard it yesterday:
"Dear Lord, we thank you for being with us during this
difficult time. When Moses and the children of Israel
were caught at the Red Sea, you didn't lead them over it,
or around it, or under it. You led them through it. And
now, in the same way, when we are in trouble, you don't

lead us over it or around it or under it. No, Lord, you lead us through it, and we thank you for that. We thank you, Lord, for our deliverance." He said "Amen" and sat down. And I said Amen in my heart.

I hope and pray that when trouble comes we will remember Moses at the Red Sea, and strengthened by that, we will go forward, trusting God to be with us and bring it out right.

5

The Moments
of Love

John 5:1-9   After this there was a feast of the Jews, and Jesus went up to Jerusalem.

Now there is in Jerusalem by the Sheep Gate a pool, in Hebrew called Beth-zatha, which has five porticoes. In these lay a multitude of invalids, blind, lame, paralyzed. One man was there, who had been ill for thirty-eight years. When Jesus saw him and knew that he had been lying there a long time, he said to him, "Do you want to be healed?" The sick man answered him, "Sir, I have no man to put me into the pool when the water is troubled, and while I am going another steps down before me." Jesus said to him, "Rise, take up your pallet, and walk." And at once the man was healed, and he took up his pallet and walked.

The Broadway play *The Elephant Man* has been acclaimed as one of the great plays of our time. During its opening season it won all the major drama awards—three Tonys, three Obies, the Drama Desk Award, the New York Drama Critics Circle Award—and has been made into a major motion picture.

The play is based on the life of John Merrick, who lived in London during the latter part of the nineteenth century. John Merrick was a horribly deformed young man. His appearance was so grotesque, his head so enormous, that he was exploited as a freak in traveling sideshows.

Early in the play, he is abandoned by Ross, his manager. Scared, lonely, and helpless, he is found by a young doctor, Frederick Treves. Treves saves him from an angry mob, gives him a home in a prestigious London hospital, treats him, educates him, and introduces him to London society. John Merrick—the Elephant Man— changes from a pathetic object of pity to an urbane and witty favorite of the aristocracy.

Watching the play recently, I was intrigued and deeply moved by the poignant scene in the underground Liverpool Street station. Robbed and deserted by Ross, Merrick is frightened, confused, abandoned.

Even now, a mob is forming. The angry crowd, panicked by his appearance, threatens to attack him. The train conductor and a policeman rush him to a room and bar the door, holding back the mob. They don't know what to do with him. They think he is an imbecile, and they treat him like one. Interestingly, in that scene, as the Elephant Man pathetically cries out for help, he says the name Jesus. They don't understand him, but when Dr. Treves arrives, Merrick is able to communicate something anyone could understand. Gurgling up from deep within his soul comes a pitiful, guttural, heart-wrenching cry—just two words, "Help me!"

As I experienced that touching moment, my mind darted back to a similar episode in the fifth chapter of John's Gospel, that dramatic scene in which Jesus healed the invalid at Bethzatha Pool.

Jesus, who appeared to be alone, since there is no mention of his disciples, had come to Jerusalem to attend one of the "feasts of obligation." In biblical times, three Jewish feasts were feasts of obligation: Passover, Pentecost, and Tabernacles. All adult male Jews who lived within fifteen miles of Jerusalem were legally bound to attend these three feasts.

Jesus made his way to the famous pool, where all the people stared with great intensity at the water, waiting expectantly for it to move. Beneath the pool was a subterranean stream which every now and then bubbled up. The belief was that the disturbance was caused by an angel, and the first person to get into the pool after the troubling of the water would be healed.

To us, this may sound like superstition. But it was the kind of belief that was widespread in ancient times. People believed in all kinds of spirits. Every tree, every river, every bush, every hill, every pool, had its resident spirit. Ancient peoples were especially impressed with the power and holiness of water. We may know water only as something that comes out of a faucet, but in the ancient world water was the most valuable, the most powerful, the most awesome of all things. Surely this notion was a factor in the origin of the rite of baptism.

When Jesus walked into that intriguing scene, his eye fell immediately upon a pitiful situation, a man who had been ill for thirty-eight years. All those years, he had watched and waited and hoped, and somehow Jesus knew the man had been there a long time.

Notice that Jesus is not pushy here. He doesn't force himself on the man. Tenderly, gently, he asks, "Do you want to be healed?" And when the lame man answers, "Oh yes, but I have no one to help me," Jesus reaches out with love. He does not fuss or argue or lecture. He meets the man where he is. He says, "Get up! Take up your bed and walk!" and the man gets up and walks away . . . and Jesus gets into trouble for healing on the sabbath.

Now, this fascinating story has, over the years, captured the imagination of poets, preachers, and theologians. All kinds of questions have been raised and analyzed: How did Jesus heal the man? What does the pool symbolize? Did the water really have medicinal powers? What about the Sheep Gate, the porches, the thirty-eight years? The healing on the sabbath? The place of this story in the Gospel of John?

These questions are interesting, but I would like to raise one more: Why didn't somebody help the man? All those years, he had waited. He said, "I have no one to help me." Why not? Thinking of this recently, I began to imagine some of the respectable excuses the people back then might have come up with to rationalize their failure to help this man who had been so needy for so long. Maybe they are the same respectable ways we excuse ourselves: Perhaps we grow accustomed to a bad situation; or we may say, "It's none of my business"; or "I don't want to get involved"; or "What can one person do?" Let's examine these excuses and see if we find ourselves somewhere between the lines.

We Grow Accustomed to a Bad Situation.

The sick man may have had no one to help him because they didn't see him anymore. He had become part of the landscape, part of the furniture, so much a part of that scene that everybody took him for granted. They had long ago ceased to think that his situation could be changed. He was as much a part of the territory as the five porches or the Sheep Gate.

We can see something so much, we can become so accustomed to seeing it as it is that we don't see it at all anymore, and thus we do nothing about it.

In 1964, I was assigned to a little church in West Tennessee. When I saw that church for the first time, I was surprised to find that while it looked clean, neat, and well-kept inside (indicating that it was much loved), the outside was drastically different. In a word, it was the most underwhelming church building I had ever seen. Built of drab, dreary, gray concrete blocks, it looked incomplete, as if when it was built the congregation had run out of money before finishing it. We found out later that that is exactly what had happened.

I asked, "Have you ever thought of painting the church?"

Some of the old-timers answered, "Oh, yes, we fully intended to paint it, but then the money ran short, so we left that undone, planning to do it after a month or so."

I asked, "When did you build? How long ago?"

They said, "Back in 1938." More than twenty-five years had passed, and they had never gotten around to it.

After a bit of silence, someone said, "I guess we just got accustomed to a bad situation. We don't notice it any more."

When we moved to Shreveport in 1972 to join the staff of The First United Methodist Church, the senior pastor asked me to walk around the church by myself. He wanted me to just look at things with a "critiquing eye" and make a note of everything I saw that needed to be changed or improved.

He said, "Be sure to do it the first week, because after you have been here a month, you may not be able to see those things any more. We need you to look at the church with fresh eyes." He was right, because, you see, we can become so accustomed to things as they are that our eyes grow stale.

This, of course, can happen not only with regard to church buildings, but even more with people situations. One of Jesus' greatest qualities was his perception. He could see things and people and situations with fresh eyes and that is why he was so loving. Love first seizes the eyes, then touches the heart, and only then extends to the hands. Real love will not let us grow accustomed to a bad situation.

It's None of My Business.

Some of the people in Jerusalem may have seen the crippled man but rationalized their inaction by saying, "I never stick my nose into other people's affairs. I don't believe in interfering in other people's lives. Anyway, maybe he doesn't want any help." Well, if helping other people is interfering, then Jesus was the Great Interferer. He walked up to Bethzatha Pool, saw the pitiful situation, refused to excuse himself, and made it his business to help the man.

The Gospels are filled with incidents in which Jesus touched people with love, making them his business, for his business was loving and caring. What if the Scriptures read like this: "Jesus saw a man blind from birth and he felt sorry for him, but did nothing because he didn't want to interfere in his life." Or "Jesus saw a man with a withered hand, and he felt bad about it but did nothing because after all it was none of his business, and besides, it was the sabbath, and he didn't want to get into trouble with the Pharisees." Of course, thank God, the Gospels don't read that way, because they are about love, and love demands that we reach out and touch other people's lives, that we make their welfare our business.

Real Christian love will not permit us to say "It's none of my business." We see that vividly in the life of Jesus.

I Don't Want to Get Involved.

How many times have you heard that excuse? How many times have you used it?

Some years ago in a respectable Chicago residential area, an elderly man was attacked—beaten and stabbed by a mugger. For some fifteen minutes, the older man screamed for help and tried desperately to defend himself. After the attacker fled, the man lay moaning and bleeding on the sidewalk for another fifteen minutes before he died.

Why bring this up in the middle of a chapter on love? Because when it was all over, the police found that the brutal murder was watched by seventeen people standing at a bus stop just across the narrow street. Not one person did anything to help!

After the man was dead and the killer gone, someone called the police. Three minutes later, police were on the scene! That elderly man might be alive today if one person of the seventeen had had enough compassion and courage to help, enough concern to call the police. When questioned later, almost every one gave the same "respectable" excuse: "I just didn't want to get involved!"

Christian love demands that we get involved. Christian love is compassionate, and compassion and action go hand in hand. It is interesting to note that in the New Testament, every time we read "Jesus was filled with compassion," we should know he is about to act, about to do something, about to become involved, about to express his love by helping somebody. Compassion and action go hand in hand. Christian love means getting involved, so this excuse doesn't hold up either.

What Can One Person Do?

Many people who saw the lame man at Bethzatha Pool might have said something like this: "Sure, I see him there. I know it's a pitiful situation. I feel really sorry for him, but what can I do? I have no power."

What *can* one person do? The answer to that is simple—a whole lot! One committed person can do unbelievable things. One person consumed with love can turn the world upside down. Jesus proved that!

Sometimes in the counseling room, while trying to help people work through difficult decisions, I will ask them to list their options and then ask which of these is the most loving thing to do.

Sometimes I ask, "What do you think Jesus would do?"

In response, many people will say, "Surely I'm not expected to act like Jesus."

But, you see, the answer to that is, "Oh, yes! That is exactly how all of us are supposed to act."

That is what makes Jesus so special. He shows us how God wants us to act, what God wants us to be, and the answer is *love*. A person who really lives in the spirit of Christ, in the spirit of love, can do unbelievable things.

In the musical *For Heaven's Sake,* Helen Kromer put it like this: "One man awake, can awaken another. . . . One man up with dawn in his eyes—multiplies."

Let me conclude by saying the obvious: *There are no respectable excuses for not loving!* As Christians, we dare not—not love! As Christians, we dare not miss this! It is the most distinctive thing in Christianity. If we fail in loving, we fail altogether.

Of course, loving and helping is risky. It got Jesus into trouble, eventually sent him to a cross, but he realized (as we must) that there is only one thing more costly than caring—and that is not caring!!

Many years ago, a young man from a very well-to-do family committed himself to loving and living in the spirit of Christ. He founded a religious order rooted in love for people, for God's creation, for all God's creatures. His name was Francis. The prayer of Saint Francis of Assisi has come to symbolize the meaning of Christian love. If only we would stop making excuses and give our energies to living its spirit:

Lord, make me an instrument of thy peace.
Where there is hatred, let me sow love;
Where there is injury, pardon;
Where there is doubt, faith;
Where there is despair, hope;
Where there is darkness, light;
Where there is sadness, joy.
O divine Master, grant that I may not so much seek
To be consoled as to console;
To be understood as to understand;
To be loved as to love.
For
It is in giving, that we receive;
It is in pardoning, that we are pardoned;
It is in dying, that we are born to eternal life.

6

The Moments of Spiritual Maturity

Matthew 5:43-48 "You have heard that it was said, 'You shall love your neighbor and hate your enemy.' But I say to you, Love your enemies and pray for those who persecute you, so that you may be sons of your Father who is in heaven; for he makes his sun rise on the evil and on the good, and sends rain on the just and on the unjust. For if you love those who love you, what reward have you? Do not even the tax collectors do the same?

And if you salute only your brethren, what more are you doing than others? Do not even the Gentiles do the same?

You, therefore, must be perfect, as your heavenly Father is perfect.

Jesus startles us in the Sermon on the Mount when he challenges us to strive for perfection. "Be perfect," he says. At first glance this instruction is hard to swallow and difficult to accept. Never would we even remotely connect ourselves with perfection. We are too vividly aware of our imperfections. They are much too glaring to miss.

But the word *perfect* here (the original Greek word was *teleos*) really means *full-grown, adult, complete, mature* (as opposed to *petty, childish, immature*). The basic idea is this: Be mature in your relationships with others. Don't be childish! Don't be self-centered! Rather, aim at godliness. Let God's grace be your measuring stick. Imitate the *unconditional love* of God. No matter what people may do to you, keep on loving them!

Our problem is that we settle for too little. We stop reaching, stop growing. We accept "childish" religion

61

rather than paying the price for "mature" faith. We are content with a chopsticks faith in a Beethoven world. Let me tell you what I mean.

Some years ago I had an interesting experience at a party. There was a house full of people, a festive mood, much noise, a hubbub of conversation and party sounds. People were standing in little clusters, and talking. Others were playing games, listening to records, watching television, or preparing refreshments in the kitchen.

In the midst of all this, I sat down at the piano, flexed my two index fingers, and began to play chopsticks—which just happens to be my complete repertoire of piano selections.

After a bit, a close friend walked over, tapped me on the shoulder, and said with a grin, "Jim, why don't you get up and let somebody play the piano who knows what she is doing?" I stood up, and he introduced a young woman who was visiting our city from another state. After some coaxing, she sat down and began to play. She was magnificent! She became one with that musical instrument. Her hands moved gracefully and confidently up and down the keyboard as she played a Beethoven masterpiece.

She was so good that everybody in the house literally dropped what they were doing. Conversation stopped, table games were pushed aside, the television was turned off, people came out of the kitchen. Everybody gathered to listen. When she finished, there was a kind of reverent silence for a brief moment . . . and then spontaneous, thunderous applause as we called for more.

Out of that experience, I had several thoughts. Was that the same piano I had been playing only moments before? What was the difference? Well, it was clear that my feeble attempt was childish, amateurish, and simplistic, while hers was studied, disciplined, dedicated, loving, masterful. Also, I had contented myself with using only two fingers and eight notes, whereas she used all her fingers and all the notes. The truth is that I had settled for just a little musical knowledge; she had obviously committed her life to it. She had trained, sacrificed, practiced, learned, and as a result had become a mature master musician.

On a deeper level, there is an interesting parallel in the world of faith. In our spiritual pilgrimage, too many of us fail to really apply ourselves. We quit too early, settle for too little. We have a "chopsticks" faith when we could have so much more. In our world today there are too many immature people and too many childish actions. I am concerned about this because I believe that childishness causes much of the misery in the world today. Friendships are destroyed, marriages disrupted, churches split, families polarized, wars started, lives lost, hearts broken—all due to spiritual and emotional childishness.

I once read a significant statement by Dr. G. B. Chisholm: "So far in the history of the world, there have never been enough mature people in the right places." This is our problem. Rather than pay the price for maturity, we are too quick to settle for childishness.

In *politics*, candidates promise "mature" leadership, and then spend the entire campaign childishly attacking the opponents with ugly smear tactics. They never get around to the real issues. There are exceptions, of course. Some are mature in their approach, but so many have become childish. A few years ago in Louisiana during a frantic governor's race, candidates were attacking each other so viciously that one man, in disgust at such childish behavior, had his name changed to None of the Above, ran for governor, and received some votes!

What about *international affairs?* One nation says to

another, "If you don't do what I want, I won't talk to you anymore!"

Or what about *entertainment?* You are driving along when suddenly, over the car radio, comes a suave voice telling about a new form of entertainment: "Not for everybody; for only the most thoughtful people—entertainment that is mature, adult, sophisticated, thought-provoking, designed for intelligent audiences." You are interested until you realize the announcer is plugging a new movie—*Sex Kittens on College Campus.* How childish we have become!

Jesus saw the dangers and problems connected with childishness, and when he said "Be perfect," at least a part of his meaning was "Grow up! Don't be like spoiled children. Don't be petty; don't be shallow. Aim at godliness; imitate the merciful, loving spirit of God. Be mature! Be fully grown up!" Let me suggest some required characteristics of spiritual maturity.

Know How to Handle Frustration.

The spiritually mature person knows how to deal with disappointments, how to turn problems into opportunities, defeats into victories. Jesus spoke that day to a frustrated people, people who were beleaguered by economic problems, heavy taxes, countless laws, oppressive government, and Roman soldiers. Jesus said to them, "Don't be childish, don't give in to hatred and resentment. Don't quit on life. Be strong! Be mature!"

Jesus knew that childish response to frustration is not only quite inadequate, but terribly dangerous. If someone does not give a little child the toy he wants, the child will scream, cry, or throw something. But put that kind of immature response on a bigger stage, and it can be dangerous, devastating.

A frightening case in point is the incident that took place in January 1980, at Kennedy Airport in New York. Just after the Soviet invasion of Afghanistan, a plane carrying Russian ambassador Dobrynin was coming in for a landing. Suddenly the Russian plane vanished from the radar screen in the Kennedy control tower. Incredibly, the plane and all the data showing its identity, altitude, and speed mysteriously disappeared.

Fortunately, one of the air-traffic control supervisors happened to be walking by, saw the information vanish, and quickly took charge. He brought the plane in safely, but in the confusion, it was brought in at the wrong altitude and through the wrong air space. Amazingly, no planes were in its path and disaster was averted.

The FBI and FAA began an immediate investigation. The conclusion seems to be that some air-traffic controller, mad at the Russians, deliberately wiped that plane off the radar screen, knowing it could crash into another plane and hundreds of people would be killed, not to mention the damage it would do to already tense Soviet-American relations. It makes you wonder, doesn't it? How many lives have been lost, how many wars started, how much harm done, by childish, immature people who have not learned how to handle frustration?

On the other side of the coin, thank God, history is filled with wonderful stories of mature people who rose above their frustrations. Milton went blind; Beethoven lost his hearing; Pasteur became a paralytic; Helen Keller was deaf, blind, and unable to speak; the apostle Paul wanted to go to Spain, but instead was thrown into a prison cell in Rome. But were those people defeated by disappointment? Absolutely not! They all turned their frustrations into instruments of victory.

We can do that too! Indeed, this is our calling, a major mark of spiritual maturity. Remember how Paul put it:

"We are troubled on every side, yet not distressed; we are perplexed, but not in despair; persecuted, but not forsaken; cast down, but not destroyed" (II Cor. 4:8-9 KJV). The spiritually mature person knows how to handle frustration.

Know How to Forgive.

How graphically the Scriptures show the quality of mercy, the spirit of forgiveness, as a godly characteristic. In Matthew, Jesus says, "Be perfect, as your heavenly Father is perfect."

Luke's Gospel renders it, "Be merciful, even as your Father is merciful" (6:36). Again and again, Jesus points out the forgiving spirit of God.

If you ever wonder, Should I forgive that person who has hurt me? just picture Jesus hanging on the cross, saying, "Father, forgive them." That is our measuring stick for forgiveness and for maturity. They betrayed him, denied him, mocked him, cursed him. They lied about him, beat him, spat upon him. They nailed him to a cross, and he forgave. That's our measuring stick. That's what God is like, and that's the way he wants us to be. The forgiving spirit is a mark of spiritual maturity.

Know How to Be Self-giving.

This is really what Jesus is getting at when he says "Be perfect." He means, "Be mature in loving others. Grow up! Stop thinking just about yourself. Reach out to others." Childish people fight for their "rights." Mature people have learned that the greatest human right is the right to be unselfish, to give of themselves, to care, to love.

The spiritually mature person also knows that the best way to express love for God is to love God's children.

Remember Paul's problem with the church at Corinth. Selfishness, factions, jealousies, were tearing the church apart. Paul wrote to them, "Put away childish things. Grow up and learn how to love. . . . The greatest of these is love."

One of the best books I have read recently is *Unconditional Love* by John Powell, a professor at Loyola University in Chicago. He ends the book with a true story about one of his students, a young man named Tommy.

Tommy was a problem. Tommy was the "atheist-in-residence" in Dr. Powell's course on theology. When he wasn't acting bored, Tommy winced, smirked, objected, or whined about the possibility of a loving God. In Dr. Powell's words, Tommy was "strange," a real pain.

At the end of the course, when Tommy turned in his final exam, he asked in a slightly cynical tone, "Do you think I'll ever find God?"

In answer to that, Dr. Powell decided to try a little shock therapy. "No!" he said very emphatically. Tommy did seem shocked as he turned to walk away.

Dr. Powell let him get about five steps away before he added, "Tommy! I don't think you'll ever find him, but I am absolutely certain that he will find you!" Tommy shrugged a little, turned, and walked out.

Tommy graduated, and some months later came a sad report: Tommy had terminal cancer. Shortly before he died, he came back to see Dr. Powell. His body was badly wasted, but his eyes were bright and his voice firm.

"It could be worse, " he said.

"Like what?" asked John Powell. Tommy explained:

Well, like being fifty and having no values or ideals, like being fifty and thinking that booze . . . and making money are the real "biggies" in life. . . .

But what I really came to see you about . . . is something you said to me on the last day of class. . . . I asked you if

you thought I would ever find God and you said,
"No!" . . . Then you said, "But he will find you." . . .

When the doctors removed a lump . . . and told me that
it was malignant, then I got serious about locating
God. . . . I really began banging bloody fists against the
bronze doors of heaven. But God did not come out. In fact,
nothing happened. . . .

I decided to spend what time I had left doing something
more profitable. . . . I remembered something else you had
said: "The essential sadness is to go through life without
loving. But it would be almost equally sad to go through life
and leave this world without ever telling those you loved that
you have loved them."

So I began with the hardest one: my Dad. He was reading
the newspaper when I approached him.

"Dad . . . "

"Yes, what?" he asked without lowering the newspaper.

"Dad, I would like to talk with you."

"Well, talk."

"I mean . . . it's really important."

The newspaper came down three slow inches. "What is
it?"

"Dad, I love you. I just wanted you to know that." . . .

The newspaper fluttered to the floor. Then my father did
two things I could never remember him ever doing before.
He cried and he hugged me. And we talked all night, even
though he had to go to work the next morning. It felt so good
to be close to my father. . . .

It was easier with my mother and little brother. . . . I was
only sorry about one thing: that I had waited so long. Here I
was, in the shadow of death, and I was just beginning to open
up to all the people I had actually been close to.

Then, one day I turned around and God was there. He
didn't come to me when I pleaded with him. . . .

But the important thing is that . . . he found me.

John Powell believes that "the surest way to find God
is . . . by opening to love," and he invited Tommy to

come to theology class to tell his story. Tommy couldn't accept that invitation, but he talked with Dr. Powell before he died.

"I'm not going to make it to your class," he said.

"I know, Tom."

"Will you tell them for me? Will you . . . tell the whole world for me?"

"I will, Tom. I'll tell them. I'll do my best."

John Powell concludes his book with these words: "So, to all of you who have been kind enough to hear this simple statement about love, thank you for listening. And to you, Tom, somewhere in the sunlit, verdant hills of heaven: I told them, Tommy . . . as best I could."

More than anything else, Jesus came to teach us how to love, how to reach out to others and love unconditionally . . . and that the greatest tragedy is not death, but to go through life without loving.

The spiritually mature person knows how to handle frustration, knows how to forgive, and knows how to love.

7

The Peacemaking Moments

Philippians 4:1-9 Therefore, my brethren, whom I love and long for, my joy and crown, stand firm thus in the Lord, my beloved.

I entreat Euodia and I entreat Syntche to agree in the Lord. And I ask you also, true yokefellow, help these women, for they have labored side by side with me in the gospel together with Clement and the rest of my fellow workers, whose names are in the book of life.

Rejoice in the Lord always; again I will say, Rejoice. Let all men know your forbearance. The Lord is at hand. Have no anxiety about anything, but in every-thing by prayer and supplication with thanksgiving let your requests be made known to God. And the peace of God, which passes all understanding, will keep your hearts and your minds in Christ Jesus.

Finally, brethren, whatever is true, whatever is honorable, whatever is just, whatever is pure, whatever is lovely, whatever is gracious, if there is any excellence, if there is anything worthy of praise, think about these things. What you have learned and received and heard and seen in me, do; and the God of peace will be with you.

Some time ago Bishop Ben Oliphint told the story of José Rodriguez, a bank robber who lived in Mexico in the golden days of the West. José would slip across the border into Texas, rob some banks, and then flee back into Mexico.

One day, a Texas Ranger caught up with José in a saloon. The Ranger put a gun to the robber's head and said, "Rodriguez, I know who you are, and if you don't give back all that money you stole from Texas banks, I'm gonna blow your head off!"

But there was a problem. José could not understand

English, and the Ranger could not speak Spanish. However, a young boy standing nearby overheard the conversation.

He said, "I will translate."

The Ranger said, "O.K. You tell him that if he doesn't give all that money back, I'm gonna blow his head off."

The boy spoke to José, and José began to shake with fear.

In Spanish, he cried out, "Don't shoot! I will tell you. No one else in the world knows where the money is. Go to the well at the north end of town. Remove the fifth brick on the far side, and there you will find the money. Don't shoot!"

The boy turned to the Texas Ranger and said in English: "José Rodriguez is a very brave man. He dares you to shoot!"

There is a sermon there somewhere, and it may have to do with the importance of communication. What we communicate can have a dramatic effect on other people. It can mean life or death, joy or sorrow; it can pick people up or knock them down. We can give peace or pain; we can be peacemakers or heartbreakers.

We have a choice: We can build up or we can tear down, and the happy people are those who realize they have that choice, and they choose to build up! This, of course, is what the seventh Beatitude is all about. When Jesus said, "Blessed are the peacemakers, for they shall be called sons of God" (Matt. 5:9), he meant, "How happy and fulfilled are the peacemakers—they shall be doing God's work." Commenting on this Beatitude, William Barclay points out:

> There are people who are always storm-centres of trouble and bitterness and strife. Wherever they are they are either involved in quarrels themselves or the cause of quarrels

between others. They are trouble-makers. There are people like that in almost every society . . . and such people are doing the devil's own work. On the other hand—thank God—there are people in whose presence bitterness cannot live, people who bridge the gulfs, and heal the breaches, and sweeten the bitternesses. Such people are doing a godlike work, for it is the great purpose of God to bring peace between men and himself, and between man and man. The man who divides men is doing the devil's work; the man who unites men is doing God's work. *(The Gospel of Matthew*, Vol. 1, Rev. Ed., Daily Study Bible Series [Philadelphia: Westminster Press, 1975], p. 110)

The choice is ours—we can be troublemakers or peacemakers. We can build up or we can tear down. In this connection, let us consider these four choices: We can encourage or we can discourage; we can soothe or we can seethe; we can laugh or we can lament; we can pardon or we can punish.

We Can Encourage or We Can Discourage.

There is a strange sentence in one of the Psalms: "I will bridle my mouth" (39:1*b*). These are the words of a man sorely tempted to spread gloom and despair and discouragement. Yet he held himself in check, knowing there was enough pessimism around, that he should rally the courage of those who felt down and out. That's good advice. The world has its share of cynics and debunkers; it is longing for words of assurance and encouragement.

When will we ever learn? People don't want to be put down; they are crying out to be lifted up.

What have you been choosing lately? The choice is ours: We can encourage or we can discourage. And it is so much better to encourage! Isn't it sad that many people have it mixed up? They have turned it completely around. They think they are divinely ordained to point out all the bad things, show us all the problems, underscore all the negatives.

Some years ago I was appointed to a church in a small town. Our family moved into the parsonage at noon. At 12:15 the doorbell rang. A member of the church felt it was her duty to come and tell me about all their problems, and especially to point out all the things the former minister had done wrong. On and on she went, spreading her message of despair and gloom and saying terrible things about her former pastor.

As I listened to her words of woe, I remember thinking three things: First, "Lady, you are telling me a lot more about yourself than about the former minister"; then I thought, "I have known him for years. He's great, and I don't believe these awful things"; and finally, "One of these days, I'm going to be leaving here, and this lady is going to be here by noon to tell my successor all about me and my faults!"

Isn't that tragic? Why do we feel that we must spread gloom? It is so much more fun to lift people up than to tear them down. Laura Huxley puts it well in *You're Not the Target:*

At one time or another the more fortunate among us make three startling discoveries:

Discovery number one: Each one of us has, in varying degree, the power to make others feel better or worse.
Discovery number two: Making others feel better is much more rewarding than making them feel worse.
Discovery number three: Making *others* feel better generally makes *us* feel better. ([New York: Farrar, Straus & Giroux, 1963], p. 3)

One of the great personalities of the early church was Barnabas, which means "son of encouragement." Barnabas was a significant leader because he lived out his name. He *was* an encourager. We in the church ought to be modern-day Barnabases—the sons and daughters of encouragement; people who listen, who care, who affirm; people who help and support one another; people who lift up and hold up and build up. But the choice is ours. We can encourage or discourage!

We Can Soothe or We Can Seethe.

There is nothing more destructive to our spirits than seething resentment. It's a spiritual cancer. It can ruin our lives, it can make us sick.

Paul Tournier, in *A Doctor's Case Book in the Light of the Bible* ([Harper & Row, 1976], pp. 149-50), tells of a woman being treated for anemia. Doctors had been working with her for months without much success. They had tried all kinds of medicines, vitamins, diet, and exercise, to no avail. As a last resort, it was decided to put her in the hospital. As she was checking in, the hospital rather routinely checked her blood. They discovered it was fine; she was well, with no sign of anemia. Miraculously, she was healed.

Intrigued by this, her doctor asked, "Has anything out of the ordinary happened in your life since your last visit?"

"Yes!" she replied. "I have suddenly been able to forgive someone against whom I bore a nasty grudge; and all at once I felt as if I could at last say 'Yes' to life!"

You see, her resentment had made her ill. When she stopped seething and decided to soothe the situation, the impact was so great, so powerful, it even changed the physical state of her blood! The choice is ours—we can encourage or discourage; we can soothe or seethe!

We Can Laugh or We Can Lament.

Some people go miserably through life, crying "Woe is me" at every turn. God meant life to be joyous. A good sense of humor has never hurt anyone, and it has made life blossom like a flower in the desert for many. Someone once said, "No one has ever been known to die of laughter." And Abraham Lincoln wrote, "If I did not laugh from time to time I would surely die." We should learn not to take ourselves so seriously; we should learn to laugh.

It is interesting to watch the bridal party at weddings. It is a nervous, emotional time, and those who know how to laugh fare much better. Some years ago I presided at a wedding that turned into a disaster because the bride had no sense of humor. She was determined to have the perfect wedding. She included everything she had ever heard of—bridesmaids, groomsmen, acolytes, altar boys, flower girls, ring bearers—the works. She tried so hard she upset everybody.

Everything went beautifully until time for the nuptial kiss. A surprise to the rest of us, the bride had asked her brother to play—of all things—a tape of "2001: A Space Odyssey." It came on with such a blast that the maid of honor jumped and knocked over a candle. As the best man tried to catch the falling candle, he stepped on the bride's dress; she dropped her flowers and her veil fell off. She stumbled as she turned to go out of the church, and the flower girl began to cry.

By the time the bride and groom reached the back of the church, she was furious. She had decided it was all his fault, and he couldn't figure out what he had done wrong. It was the only time in my life I have taken a bride and groom into a private room to calm them down before they could even go to the reception.

I said: "Look, you are married. That's all that matters. You love each other and want to share your life together, and you are just as married as any couple that's ever taken those sacred vows. That's what it's all about! All the candles and pageantry—that's just frosting on the cake. There are no perfect weddings, and the things that went wrong are just things to laugh about in years to come. You love each other, and you are married—that's the important thing."

Another couple I know had one of the most unusual wedding experiences ever. We accidentally scheduled the ceremony on the day of a big parade. The streets were blocked off, and at the appointed time, there was no congregation. The guests couldn't get to the church because of the parade, so we had to delay the wedding a full hour.

What do we do when things like that happen? Well, we can laugh or we can lament! That great couple decided to laugh. Their sense of humor got them through. They went out and had their pictures made with the bands, and they still joke that they had a parade with seventeen marching bands at their wedding!

Or what about the couple that married in Arkansas? The minister asked the groom, "Will you have this woman to be your wedded wife, to live together in the holy estate of matrimony? Will you love her, comfort her, honor and keep her in sickness and in health; and forsaking all others, keep you only unto her, so long as you both shall live?"

The groom was so nervous he said, "Would you repeat the question?"

It took a sense of humor to get through that! They have it on tape, and every now and then, to this day, they listen to it and laugh!

What do you think? The choice is ours. We can

encourage or discourage; we can soothe or seethe; we can laugh or lament.

We Can Pardon or We Can Punish.

Why do we think we need to punish people? I saw a bumper sticker the other day that made me ill: "I don't get mad, I get even." Isn't that pathetic?

Some time ago a man came by to see me. He was depressed and despondent. He and his wife were having problems. They had gone to Dallas the weekend before to celebrate their anniversary. As they were heading out of town, he remembered something he had forgotten to take care of at his office. He turned back, made the necessary arrangements, and they were on their way again, having lost only fifteen minutes.

For some reason, the stop had made his wife furious. They drove to Dallas in silence. They endured a miserable weekend. She refused to speak to him. When he tried to touch her, she pushed him away. A week had passed when he came to see me.

"She still won't speak to me. She won't listen to reason. She is still punishing me."

Isn't that sad? Why do we punish people? Why do we punish those we love in such cruel ways? It is so useless. It is so senseless! It is much better to pardon, much better to forgive, much better to be a peacemaker!

The choice is ours—we can encourage or discourage, soothe or seethe, laugh or lament, pardon or punish.

8

The Moments of Commitment

Luke 9:57-62 As they were going along the road, a man said to him, "I will follow you wherever you go." And Jesus said to him, "Foxes have holes, and birds of the air have nests; but the Son of man has nowhere to lay his head." To another he said, "Follow me." But he said, "Lord, let me first go and bury my father." But he said to him, "Leave the dead to bury their own dead; but as for you, go and proclaim the kingdom of God." Another said, "I will follow you, Lord, but let me first say farewell to those at my home." Jesus said to him, "No one who puts his hand to the plow and looks back is fit for the kingdom of God."

I n the ninth chapter of Luke's Gospel, we discover a disturbing passage of Scripture in which Jesus actually turns away three men who want to be disciples. This is bothersome because it seems so out of character for Jesus to discourage these would-be followers. Why did Jesus turn them away? What can this mean?

It probably means that Jesus saw through the men. He was very good at that. How perceptive he was! He saw immediately the loneliness of Zacchaeus, the mixed-up priorities of the rich young ruler, and he quickly sensed that the lawyers would try to trip him up with loaded questions.

And somehow he sensed that these three men were not totally committed. Each, in his own way, wanted to put certain conditions on his discipleship. But Jesus knew that kind of conditional discipleship would not work. They were heading toward a showdown in Jerusalem!

The *first man* sounds good. Maybe that's the problem; he sounds *too* good. He talks a good game, but Jesus senses that he is not ready to make the sacrifices demanded by discipleship. He is not really ready for the action that looms ahead in Jerusalem.

Jesus' answer to the *second man*, "Let the dead bury the dead," seems at first glance to be harsh. Upon closer examination, however, we realize why Jesus answered as he did. If the man's father were already dead, what's he doing out here on the roadside? The man is really saying, "I will follow you *after* my father has died." This might be a year, or five years, or ten, or twenty. The man has missed the urgency of the moment, the urgency of the call. Only a short time before, Jesus had "set his face toward Jerusalem." At the very moment of this encounter, he is on his way to the cross. This is serious business, and he senses that the second man is not ready to totally commit himself. He does not really understand how important, how urgent the whole matter is.

When the *third man* says, "Let me first say farewell to those at my home," Jesus evidently recognizes that he is not ready to break with the past. We miss the point if we think Jesus is attacking family life. Certainly not! Not at all! No, somehow Jesus has sensed, either through the tone of voice, the shifting eyes, or the awkward indecision, that it is not this man's family that is holding him back. It is his own hesitation, his own inability to break with the past. Thus bound by the old, he misses the new.

We have here a quickly drawn portrait of three men toying with discipleship, but *not totally committed*. Each in his own way wants to put certain conditions on that commitment. But it won't work, will it? The call is to *unconditional commitment*, commitment with no strings attached!

A young woman walked into our church recently. She looked tired, worried. She was actually slumped over as if carrying a heavy load.

"What's the matter?" I said to her. "You look as if you are carrying all the troubles of the world on your back."

"No," she replied sadly, "not *all* the troubles. The truth is I just have one problem. My problem is that I am not really committed to anything!"

What about us? Could that be our problem? Are we totally committed, committed without reservation to God . . . or to anyone . . . or anything?

A few weeks ago I conducted a funeral service for one of the finest men I have ever known. He died at the age of eighty-four. The person who coined the word *gentleman* must have had someone like him in mind, because he was a *gentle* man. But at the same time, he had a tenacious sense of commitment. He was totally committed to his wife for more than sixty years. He was totally committed to his church. He was totally committed to God.

A couple of months before his death, he lost his sight. I went to minister to him, and he ministered to me. I was inspired by his response to blindness.

He said, "For more than eighty years I have been able to see the beauties and wonders of God's creation. I had my sight and now I have lost it. Blessed be the name of the Lord!"

That is total commitment—commitment without conditions. It's the stuff great people are made of. It's Job, crying out in the midst of great pain: "Though he slay me, yet will I trust him." It's Susanna Wesley, calling her children to her deathbed: "Children, as soon as I am released, sing a psalm of praise to God." It's the apostle Paul, writing from his prison cell: "Rejoice with me; again, I say, rejoice. For me to live is Christ and to die is gain."

Total commitment. Commitment without conditions—
that is our calling as Christian people. That is the spirit in
which we, as disciples, are to live daily, and it includes
these three qualities: *unconditional gratitude, unconditional surrender, unconditional love.*

The Spirit of Unconditional Gratitude

Commitment to God means living daily in a spirit of
gratitude that is not measured or calculated, gratitude
with no strings, thanksgiving with no conditions attached.
Real gratitude is not dependent upon circumstances or on
the number of things we possess. Real gratitude involves
more than counting material blessings. Now I hope you
will count your blessings, but remember that as
Christians, even if we don't have many possessions, we
can still be grateful because God is with us and he is for us.
He is our friend, and that is the real source of
thanksgiving. That's the real reason we can be grateful.

Isn't it fascinating to note that our greatest expressions
of thanksgiving came from people who did not have a lot
of material things:

• Jesus had no place to lay his head.
• Luther was in hiding for his life.
• Francis of Assisi was voluntarily poor.
• Helen Keller was blind and deaf.
• Mother Teresa lives in a leper colony.
• The pilgrims were hungry and cold.

Unconditional gratitude, gratitude with no strings
attached—that was their watchword because they knew
God was with them. Life was hard, times were tough, but
God was with them, and that's all that mattered!

Back in the early days of the church, a rather strong-smelling incense was burned in the worship services, and the aroma would saturate the clothing of all those present. When they left, they literally smelled of incense. People could tell by their fragrance that they had been to church, in the presence of God. Isn't that great? The aroma of the totally committed Christian is unconditional gratitude, gratitude under all circumstances. It is one of the main qualities of total commitment.

The Spirit of Unconditional Surrender

Don't let the word *surrender* throw you. I would like for us to reclaim the word as it was used originally in the New Testament. Unfortunately, it has taken on a narrow, negative tone and now most often denotes *weakness, defeat, giving up*.

I heard about a little boy who, when he was asked to describe Christians, said, "Christians are mild, weak, quiet people who never fight or talk back." Then he added, "Daddy is a Christian. But Mother isn't."

Sounds like Dad had given up, but that is not what the word *surrender* meant in the New Testament. Men and women who were courageous, powerful, and outspoken were referred to as *surrendered people*, for in the Scriptures, *surrender* does not mean *defeat*. It means:

- *obedience* to God's will;
- *cooperation* with God's purposes;
- *submission* to God's direction;
- *commitment* to God's cause.

Some years ago when the great Christian Kagawa was on a speaking tour, he was asked by a college student to define *prayer*. The audience fully expected him to give a highly theological explanation, but he surprised them by defining prayer with one word—*surrender*.

If *surrender* still bothers you, then use the word *trust*. It's the same thing, and it is most poignantly expressed in the Garden of Gethsemane as Jesus says, "Not my will, Father, but thine be done." "Thy will be done"—that is unconditional surrender, and it is a basic ingredient in total commitment.

The Spirit of Unconditional Love

This is *agape*—uncalculated goodwill for all people, unselfish love, love in all circumstances, love with no strings attached, unfettered love, love with no conditions. More than anything, this is what Jesus came to teach us: *how to love unconditionally*. In Jesus, we see what God is like. In him, God is saying, "Look! This is how I love all of you—my love is unconditional. Nothing you can do will stop me from loving you! You can betray me, deny me, taunt me, beat me, curse me, spit on me, nail me to a cross, and I will keep on loving you. There is nothing you can do to me that will stop me from loving you. I love you—unconditionally!"

And that is the way God wants us to love one another! I can't say, "I will love you if you are good to me" or "I will love you if you love me back." I can't say that and live in the spirit of Christ. I can live in his spirit only by loving unconditionally, expecting nothing in return, loving unselfishly.

Robert E. Lee was once asked his opinion of a certain man. General Lee responded, "He is a fine and able man, and I commend him to you highly!"

"But General," the questioner protested, "don't you know the terrible things this man says about you?"

"Yes," Lee answered, "I know, but you didn't ask how he felt about *me*. You asked what I think of him, and I think he is a fine and able man, and I commend him to you highly."

That is unconditional love, and it is our calling as Christian disciples. What is total commitment? It is unconditional gratitude in all circumstances, unconditional surrender to God's will, unconditional love for all people.

9

The Moments of Spiritual Growth

I Corinthians 13 If I speak in the tongues of men and of angels, but have not love, I am a noisy gong or a clanging cymbal. And if I have prophetic powers, and understand all mysteries and all knowledge, and if I have all faith, so as to remove mountains, but have not love, I am nothing. If I give away all I have, and if I deliver my body to be burned, but have not love, I gain nothing.

Love is patient and kind; love is not jealous or boastful; it is not arrogant or rude. Love does not insist on its own way; it is not irritable or resentful; it does not rejoice at wrong, but rejoices in the right. Love bears all things, believes all things, hopes all things, endures all things.

Love never ends; as for prophecies, they will pass away; as for tongues, they will cease; as for knowledge, it will pass away. For our knowledge is imperfect and our prophecy is imperfect; but when the perfect comes the imperfect will pass away. When I was a child, I reasoned like a child; when I became a man, I gave up childish ways. For now we see in a mirror dimly, but then face to face. Now I know in part; then I shall understand fully, even as I have been fully understood. So faith, hope, love abide, these three; but the greatest of these is love.

A few years ago a leading newspaper ran a story about a music test given to some students in an unidentified junior high school. When you read some of these fascinating answers, you will understand why that school is still, to this very day, unidentified:

"Music sung by two people at the same time is called a duel."
"A xylophone is an instrument used mainly to illustrate the letter X."
"Dirges are music written to be played at sad, sad occasions, such as funerals, weddings, and the like."

"*Refrain* means 'don't do it!' A refrain in music is the part you
    better not try to sing."
"A virtuoso is a musician with real high morals."
"J. S. Bach died from 1750 to the present day."
"I know what a sextet is, but I'd rather not say."
"Handel was half German, half Italian, and half English. He
    was rather large!"

Now, we can tell from the results of this test that right
answers are important. But have you stopped to think
that right *questions* are important, too? I would like to
discuss what I think is a "right" question, a significant
question: What is the responsibility of the church to our
society, or to our nation? There are many answers to that
question because there are many responsibilities.

One of the church's responsibilities is to produce
mature people, people who are *spiritually* mature. In
growing up, we normally pass through three stages,
which we will call the Childish Stage, the Adolescent
Stage, and the Mature Adult Stage.

- In the Childish Stage, the cry is: "Do something for
  me!"
- In the Adolescent Stage, the cry is: "Leave me
  alone! I can do it myself!"
- In the Mature Adult Stage, the cry is: "Let me do
  something for you!"

Let us examine the unique characteristics of each of these
stages:

The Childish Stage

The key word here is *selfishness*, immature disregard
for others. Paul put it like this: "When I was a child, I

spoke like a child, I thought like a child, I reasoned like a child; when I became a man, I gave up childish ways" (13:11).

Life brings no greater blessing than a child, obviously; children are wonderful. But it is a heartbreaking tragedy when a child never develops physically, mentally, socially, emotionally, or spiritually. Some people never mature. In *The Miracle of Love,* Charles Allen points out several childish characteristics, which might apply also to those people:

> Children become very upset over any personal hurt. If pins prick the flesh, they will cry as if deadly wounded. They are not the most concerned about the suffering of others, they weep mostly for themselves.
>
> Children want to be the center of attention. They are jealous of all about them. They are willing to play, if they can choose the game. They demand applause and appreciation.
>
> Children have to be taught to be thankful. Gratitude for them does not come naturally. They take all the blessings of life as a matter of course.
>
> Children owe nobody anything. Their attitude is to get all they can but they have little obligation to any person. They rarely think of what they owe their parents or the society in which they live.
>
> Children are completely self-centered. They live in a world that revolves around themselves. ([Old Tappan, N.J.: Fleming H. Revell, 1972], pp. 44-45)

Childish people are petty, and pettiness is immature selfishness. The cry of the childish person is, "Do something for me! Help me! Give me something!"

The Adolescent Stage

Here the key word is *arrogant,* but other descriptive adjectives fly fast and furious—rebellious, restless, discontented, ruthless, prideful. Adolescent people never grew up. In trying to cut the apron strings, they went overboard, let the pendulum swing too far, and have become hostile and resentful of authority.

They are scared to death, but they try to cover up by saying things like: "I don't answer to anybody; I'm my own boss. Nobody's gonna tell me what to do. Nobody's gonna tell me how to behave. My life's my own and I'll do as I please. You gotta look out for Number One. I know what I want out of life, and nobody is going to stop me. I'm a self-made person. I don't need anybody." Adolescent people say these kinds of things over and over, and so loudly that you wonder who they are trying to convince. As a biblical illustration of the adolescent stage, listen to Adam and Eve: "Who does God think he is—telling us what we can eat and what we can't?"

Adolescent-stage people are arrogant; their cry is, "Leave me alone! I can take care of myself!"

The Mature Adult Stage

When I reached "The Big 4–0," a "friend" of mine put on my desk a sheet of paper describing life after forty:

YOU KNOW YOU'RE GROWING OLDER . . .

When most everything hurts and what doesn't hurt doesn't work;

When you feel like the night before and you haven't been anywhere;

When your little black book contains only names ending in M.D.;

When you get winded playing chess;

When you join a health club and don't go;

When you sit in a rocking chair and can't get it going;

When your knees buckle and your belt won't;

When dialing long distance wears you out;
When your back goes out more than you do;
When a fortune teller offers to read your face;
When your pacemaker makes the garage door go up when
  you see a pretty girl walk by.

These may be signs of growing older, but they are not signs of maturity. Growing older does not necessarily mean that we become mature. Some people live a long time, but they never grow up.

On the other hand, some who have not lived for many years are quite mature. The key word, the measuring stick for maturity, is *love*—humble service, gracious thoughtfulness. If you want to test your maturity, test how loving you are.

The mature person is big-spirited, magnanimous, tender, concerned, committed to others in goodwill. When the mature adult weeps, it is most often for others. The mature adult appreciates approval, but works on even when there is no recognition. The mature adult is saturated with the spirit of gratitude, filled with the spirit of compassion.

It is interesting to note that both Jesus and Paul equated maturity with love. Jesus said, "Be merciful like God." Paul said, "The greatest of these [the most mature of these] is love." The most mature person is the person most able to be loving; the cry here is, "Let me do something for you; let me be a servant, let me help you; let me be a friend and a neighbor and a servant to others."

We see these three approaches to life dramatically expressed in the story of the prodigal son. At first, he selfishly demands, "Give me my inheritance now! I don't want to wait around until you die." How childish!

Then he moves into the adolescent stage—he runs away. As he walks down the road, he says, "I'm my own boss, I'm Number One. I'm not answering to anybody anymore. I can make it all by myself; I don't need anybody." How adolescent!

But he squandered his money in riotous living and became a feeder of pigs. For a Jewish boy, that was the depths of degradation. You can't get any lower than that. That was the "two-by-four" that got his attention! "He came to himself," the Scriptures put it. He matured! He returned home and said humbly, "Father, make me a servant. I'm no longer worthy to be your son. Make me a hired servant." He had grown up!

And, in these three stages, we see the way people relate to life today—the way they relate to the church, to marriage, to work, to school, to others, to God, to the nation:

THE CHURCH. Some people relate to the church childishly: "I will come to church as long as you please me. I'll participate as long as you let me sit where I want to sit, as long as I get the choir robe I want, I like the hymns we sing, the preacher says what I want to hear, the teacher teaches what I want. I'll come as long as you make me happy. But if anyone crosses me, if anyone does something I don't like, I'll quit. I'll take my tricycle and go home!" How childish!

Some relate to the church in an adolescent way: "I don't need the church. I surely don't need to go to Sunday school. That's for kids and old folks, not for me. I'm gonna live my life out here in the far country, doing my own thing. I have three cars and a boat; why would I need the church?" How adolescent!

Then (thank God) there are some in the church who are mature adults: "Let me be the church for others! Let me be part of the continuing ministry of Christ. Lord, make me the instrument of your love and peace."

MARRIAGE. Some come to marriage like little children: "I'll stay married to you as long as you make me happy. If you do what I want you to do, if you please me—act like I want you to act, say what I want you to say—if you make me happy, I'll stay married to you. But if you don't, I'll get me another playmate!"

Others are adolescent in their approach: "I'll marry you, but I won't answer to you or anybody. I want three nights out each week with no questions asked. I don't have to answer to you. Nobody owns me. Who do you think you are, asking me where I've been?"

Then, thank God, some come to marriage like adults: "Let me love you, please let me love you." But too many people spend too much time trying to find the right person and too little time learning to *be* the right person.

THE NATION. Some people approach government, the nation, and society childishly: "What's in it for me? Where's the loophole? Where's the handout?" Others are like adolescents: "I won't participate in government. I'm not going to get involved. I'll sit on the sidelines and criticize, but don't expect me to work to make this world a better place." But then there are the mature adults: "Let me do my part to make our nation great." This is what John Kennedy meant when he said, "Ask not what your country can do for you, but what you can do for your country."

This is the way some people relate to work, the way they relate to school, the way they relate to other people, and the way they relate to God.

GOD. The way we relate to God is gauged by our prayer life. Are we childish in our praying? Do we come to God saying, "Lord, give me this or that. Lord, do this for me. Bless me, give to me." Are we adolescent in our approach, saying, "Who needs to pray? It's just words. I can make it by myself. I don't need God or anybody."

But some are mature adults. They pray, "Lord, use me; make me a servant. Make me an instrument of your peace. Where there is hatred, let me sow love; where there is injury, let me bring pardon; where there is doubt, let me cultivate faith; where there is despair, let me instill hope; where there is darkness, let me light a candle." Thank God for mature people who pray like that and live like that. Let me conclude with two quick observations:

First, don't categorize people. Don't worry about who is childish and who is adolescent, and who is mature. Because the truth is, all these potentials reside in each of us. At any given moment I can be childish, or adolescent, or I can be mature.

Second, the Christian faith says something very simple to us. It says grow up! Be mature. And the way to grow up is to learn how to become more loving. That's what it's all about.

10

The Moments of Life

John 10:10 The thief comes only to steal and kill and destroy; I came that they may have life, and have it abundantly.

H ow can we tell if someone is dead or alive? What are the reliable signs of death—or of life? To prime the pump of our thinking, let's consider these three vignettes:

Some years ago one of our United Methodist bishops died, and another bishop was called upon to preside at the funeral. Somehow the newspaper made a terrible mistake. They accidentally reversed the bishops and printed the wrong obituary. When the presiding bishop saw the inadvertent announcement of his own death, he was understandably concerned. He was especially afraid that his son, who was away at college, might see the bogus obituary.

Quickly, he made a long distance call: "I'm so glad I caught you. Did you see in the morning paper the report that I had died?"

The son answered as only a college student could: "Sure did, Dad. By the way, where are you calling from?"

Next, remember with me one of the most bizarre events of 1983. A young woman was found lying unconscious on the floor of her home. She was pronounced dead and left lying there for a couple of hours as police officers investigated the cause of her death. Finally, after her body was taken to the city morgue and placed on a table for an autopsy, a police detective noticed

95

that she was swallowing, and she was rushed to a nearby hospital and revived. It seems she had taken medication that had caused a body temperature so extreme that her breathing was suspended and her pulse undetectable. They thought she was dead, but today she is alive and well!

Then there was the woman who took my hand as we stood in the small intensive care unit beside the silent and still figure of her husband. Tears misted our eyes as we looked down on the emaciated body of this man with whom she had shared a very special love for more than fifty years. He had been in the hospital for months, unable to communicate for several weeks. Now he was hooked up to all kinds of machines that were keeping him alive—one helped him breathe, another kept his heart going, still another fed him.

Suddenly she broke the silence. "That's not really my husband," she said. "That's just the worn-out body that housed his spirit. They're keeping the vital things going, as I suppose they must, but I've already given him up. I've already released him. I decided several days ago that those machines are working, but really, he is gone."

What do you think? Was he gone? Was she right? When is a person considered really dead? What is the thin line that distinguishes between life and death? What are the signs? Is it when the heart stops? Is it when the brain waves cease? Is it when there is no breath? And are the definitions of physical death related in any way to the symptoms of spiritual death?

Ever since the celebrated case of Karen Ann Quinlan, we have wondered and debated about the ethics involved in keeping patients alive with machines—or in "pulling the plug." Should we pull the plug? If so, when should we pull it? And who will do it?

These are hard questions. In earlier days, it was much

simpler. They just held a mirror up to a person's face. If no evidence of breath appeared on the mirror, the person was pronounced dead. But now a respirator may prolong the process indefinitely. Now it is more complex, more confusing, more difficult.

What do you think? When is a person really dead? Over the years the major evidences of death have indeed been these three basic definitions: no heartbeat, no brain activity, no breath. Interestingly, in the Cairo museum in Egypt, alongside the mummies of some of the more powerful Pharaohs are placed three urns. Inside the urns are the vital organs of the Pharaoh: his heart in one, his brain in another, his lungs in the third. Thus even in ancient Egypt, heart, brain, and lung activity were considered the vital signs of life. The absence of these three meant death.

In recent years we have added a fourth sign of death. Bill Hull speaks of this in his paper, "When Are You Really Dead?" In addition to the three we have mentioned, Dr. Hull suggests this fourth sign—"when machines or other external devices are required to sustain life artificially."

With this as a backdrop, I suggest that these four symptoms—no life apart from external machines, no heartbeat, no brain activity, no breath—are also the precise symptoms of spiritual death. That is, when faith is fully dependent on somebody else or on the external machine of religion; when faith loses its heartbeat of concern for others; when faith stops stretching the brain and challenging the mind; or when faith loses the Spirit-breath of God—then we are in trouble. We are spiritually dead!

The good news of our faith however, is resurrection! We can come alive again. God can reawaken the vital signs of life within us. Let's look at each of these signs of death, in the hope that as we do, we might find that which makes for abundant life.

Those Who Require External Machinery

These people never think for themselves. They never have intense feelings or do anything creative. They just go along, their faith sustained only by what they draw from others. There is no inner strength—no inner poise, no strength of character, no personal prayer life, no unbending commitment, no unwavering values, no sense of conscience, no well-thought-out philosophy of life, no private celebration of God's presence. They merely attach themselves to some person or group, or rigidly go through the motions dictated by the religious institution to which they belong. If the plug were pulled, their faith would wither and die because it has no inner vitality of its own.

Please don't misunderstand me. We all need help from others. We need good churches to train and inspire us. We need mothers and fathers to show us the way. We need good leaders to challenge us. We need the external symbols, acts, liturgies, and rituals of the church. We need a community of faith to encourage us and comfort us. But we also need our own personal faith. We need our own unique encounter with the Living Lord. We need a faith within, an inner faith that can sustain us even if the plug is pulled.

There is a fascinating example of this in the Old Testament. The prophet Jeremiah sees it coming: Jerusalem is going to fall. The Temple, the Holy City—the external machinery—will be destroyed. The people will be taken away as exiles into a foreign land. The Babylonians were about to pull their religious plug. And

Jeremiah cried out, "It's not enough to have the law of God written on tablets of stone. External machinery won't work now; we need a new covenant, written within."

When we have our own strong inner faith, then every place can be a holy place, every bush a burning bush, every job a sacred task, every moment a celebration of God's presence, and every problem can be an opportunity. When we have our own strong inner faith, we can be contributors to the community of faith—not just parasites who hang on until someone pulls the plug.

Those Whose Faith Has No Heartbeat

These people have no compassion, no concern for others, no sense of mission or service, no love. They think only of themselves. Perhaps knocked about by the problems of life, the troubles of the world, they have become cynical, calloused, and critical, cold and calculating. They don't want to be their brothers' keepers, or even their brothers' brothers or sisters.

This was the rich young ruler's problem: "I want eternal life for myself, but don't expect me to bother with other people!" This was the elder brother's problem: "You never did anything for me! But now this other son has come home and you've called for a great celebration. Well, don't expect me to rejoice! Don't expect me to welcome him home with open arms! Don't expect me to forgive and forget."

The hardhearted elder brother—put a spiritual stethoscope to his heart and the beat will be pretty faint, if indeed it can be heard at all. As the song put it, "You gotta have heart!" We "gotta have love," or we are spiritually dead. Unfortunately, some people never learn that.

Those Whose "Faith Brain Waves" Have Stopped

These are the people who stop growing, stop stretching, stop thinking, stop learning. A disciple is a learner. Sometimes people forget that; they close their minds. A brain scan of their spiritual thoughts would show that all the lines are perfectly still!

Remember the answer of the elderly gentleman when a reporter commented, "You mean you have lived one hundred years on the face of this earth!? My goodness, in that time I imagine you have seen lots of changes!"

The oldtimer replied, "I sure have, and I've been against every one of 'em!" That's the sin of the closed mind.

Jesus came, introducing changes that needed to be made, but the closed-minded people of the first century were against every one of them. They didn't want to be bothered, they didn't want to think, they didn't want their brains disturbed or made active, and they tried to silence him with a cross.

In my opinion, nothing was more responsible for putting Jesus on the cross than closed-mindedness—no brain activity. It is indeed a sign of spiritual death.

Those Who Have No Breath

Breath is the symbol for the Spirit of God. The Old Testament Hebrew word for breath is *ruach*, the same word used for God's Spirit. The New Testament Greek word for breath is *pneuma*, the same word used for God's Spirit. God breathed life into a human being in the Garden of Eden. At Pentecost, the Spirit came with the rush of a mighty wind—the breath of God blew on that place.

Has anyone ever seen or felt the Spirit-breath of God in

us? I wonder if anyone, anywhere, has ever looked at you or me and somehow caught a glimpse of the Spirit of God. If not, we may be spiritual corpses.

Someone once said that the best Christian is the one who reminds people of the Spirit of Christ. Do people ever see the Spirittore of Christ in us? Do they ever feel the Spirit-breath of God in us? If we were to have a spiritual checkup today, how would we stack up? Could we make it, apart from the external machinery of religion? Do we have a healthy, loving heartbeat of concern for others? Do we have active brain waves that grow spiritually every day? Do we have in us the Spirit-breath of God? It's something to think about, isn't it?

11

The Moments of Kindness

Ephesians 4:25-32 Therefore, putting away falsehood, let every one speak the truth with his neighbor, for we are members one of another. Be angry but do not sin; do not let the sun go down on your anger, and give no opportunity to the devil. Let the thief no longer steal, but rather let him labor, doing honest work with his hands, so that he may be able to give to those in need. Let no evil talk come out of your mouths, but only such as is good for edifying, as fits the occasion, that it may impart grace to those who hear.

And do not grieve the Holy Spirit of God, in whom you were sealed for the day of redemption. Let all bitterness and wrath and anger and clamor and slander be put away from you, with all malice, and be kind to one another, tenderhearted, forgiving one another, as God in Christ forgave you.

Some years ago when I was a seminary student, I served a church in a beautiful little village in Ohio. One summer afternoon, on the main street of that town, I drove into one of the most memorable experiences of my life.

It was raining steadily. Just ahead of me, a little girl, who looked to be about eight or nine years old, lost control of her bicycle on the rain-slick street and crashed to the pavement, scraping her knee and spilling a sack full of groceries in the street. I did what anyone would do. I stopped to help.

She cried quietly as I cleaned her injured knee and helped gather up the scattered groceries, then willingly accepted my offer to drive her home. We deposited the soggy groceries in the back seat and placed her bike in the trunk. Following her directions, we arrived at her home in a few minutes. Her mother was most gracious and appreciative—until she found out who I was.

When I said I was the new minister in town, her mood changed abruptly. She became nervous, appeared almost frightened, and began to beg me to leave. She blurted out that her husband, who was due home any moment, didn't like ministers and would not permit them in the house. Early in life he evidently had some bad experience which had caused him to despise the church.

As his wife told me of his hostility, I noticed that on the wall were pictures of her husband as a champion boxer—a huge man with monstrous arms and fierce eyes. Even as I looked at his pictures and the trophies and ribbons displayed there, I too had a sudden mood change. I decided it probably would be a good idea for me to leave before he got home!

But it was too late. He was coming in the front door. Nervously, his wife stammered out an introduction.

As soon as he heard I was a minister, he glared at me. "Get out and don't ever come back. No one from the church is wanted here. No minister is welcome here. Get out right now!"

His wife looked at the floor, embarrassed, and I did what anyone in his right mind would do: I said "I'm sorry" and left.

Next Sunday morning during the first hymn, I couldn't believe my eyes. That man slipped into the back of the church and took a seat on the last pew. A shocked murmur slid across the congregation, a few gasps, numerous whispers, lots of raised eyebrows. I gulped a couple of times myself. During the last hymn he slipped quietly out.

I didn't see him again until the next Sunday. He returned, and at the end of the service came to the altar

and joined the church on profession of faith. It was a
touching moment. People were moved to tears.

And I was moved to curiosity. Which sermon had
touched him? This Sunday's, or the one before? What had
broken through that hard shell of hostility? I had to know!

His answer caught me off guard. "I hate to tell you this,
but it wasn't either of your sermons. It wasn't anything
you said."

"Well, what was it?" I asked.

I'll never forget his answer: "You were kind to my little
girl. That's what got my attention. You were kind to my
daughter."

I learned a valuable lesson that day—a lesson about the
importance of kindness. In fact, one of the most
significant and impressive signs of Christian faith is
kindness. We don't need to be thoughtless or arrogant or
rude or harsh or preoccupied or hateful. We can choose to
be kind. You see, we may master church history, speak
high-sounding theological phrases, quote the great
philosophers, even commit to memory large blocks of
Scripture, but only when we show people genuine
kindness do they really begin to see our faith.

If you want to be an effective witness for God, if you
want to show forth the Spirit of Christ, if you want to help
your church, then be a kind person; be kind to everyone
you meet.

Some people never learn that. They go through life
pushing and shoving and grabbing, thinking only of
themselves, only of what they want. They seem never to
realize how much that attitude turns people off and drives
them away. Shel Silverstein emphasizes this in *Where the
Sidewalk Ends*, with a poem called "My Rules":

If you want to marry me, here's what you'll have to do:
You must learn how to make a perfect
    chicken dumpling stew.

And you must sew my holey socks,
   and soothe my troubled mind,
And develop the knack for scratching my back,
And keep my shoes spotlessly shined.
And while I rest you must rake up the leaves,
And when it is hailing and snowing
You must shovel the walk . . . and be still when I talk,
And—hey!—where are you going?

That poem reminds me of Maslow's famous quote: "If the only tool you have is a hammer, you tend to treat everything as if it were a nail." Does that sound at all familiar? Do you know someone whose only tool is a hammer, so they tend to try to smash everyone? But, you see, the hammer is not our only tool. We don't need to negotiate from power. We can use the tool of loving-kindness.

How important it is that we in the church learn to cultivate the attitude of kindness! Our kindness may be the only sermon some person out there will ever hear. The Christian is kind. We are called to imitate the kindness of our Lord. Poet John Boyle O'Reilly expressed this in "What Is Good":

    "What is real good?"
     I asked in musing mood.
    "Order," said the law court;
     "Knowledge," said the school;
    "Truth," said the wise man;
     "Pleasure," said the fool;
    "Love," said the maiden;
     "Beauty," said the page;
    "Freedom," said the dreamer;
     "Home," said the sage;
    "Fame," said the soldier;
     "Equity," the seer.
    Spake my heart full sadly

> "The answer is not here."
> Then within my bosom
> Softly this I heard;
> "Each heart holds the secret,
> Kindness is the word."

We can be kind if we choose to be, and if Christ is really in us, we will be!

In Ephesians 4:32, a wonderful verse not only reflects the importance of kindness, but reveals three different levels of kindness: "Be kind to one another [the level of common courtesy], tenderhearted [the level of empathy], forgiving one another, as God in Christ forgave you [the level of Christlike kindness]." Let's look at each of these levels; we may find ourselves somewhere between the lines:

The Level of Common Courtesy

"Be kind to one another" is the way the writer puts it—treat one another with courtesy.

Just the other day I did something that displeased the driver behind me. He honked his horn angrily and shook his fist and shouted some theological words in a nontheological context! I felt hurt, rejected, abused, and maybe I deserved it; but I yearned for kindness, understanding, common courtesy.

You have heard the old saying, Sticks and stones may break my bones, but words will never hurt me. But it isn't true, is it? Words do hurt. Our worst hurts, our deepest wounds, come from words—harsh, angry, cruel words, hateful words, unkind, discourteous words.

Some people think common courtesy is becoming less common in our culture, and we all are the losers if this be the case. I must say that some of the slogans characteristic of our time bother me: "Look out for yourself at someone else's expense." "Develop clout. Use your strength to get what you want." "Do to others before they do to you." "I've got mine; too bad about yours!" "Negotiate from power!" "I don't get mad; I get even!"

Somehow these ideas seem not only contrary to common courtesy, but diametrically opposed to the Spirit of Christ, for our model is a kind man who went about doing good, helping and caring for others—not a bully who intimidated people to get his way. Even when he cleansed the Temple so powerfully and dramatically, he was thinking of others. He upset the tables because he was angry about the hurts of other people. People were being oppressed, and Jesus didn't like that.

We must remember that courtesy, however, is much more than using the proper rules of etiquette. It's major thrust is that we show love and respect for others. The children's poem "I'm Making a List," by Shel Silverstein, shows that we sometimes forget this:

> I'm making a list of the things I must say
> for politeness,
> And goodness and kindness and gentleness,
> sweetness and rightness:
> > Hello
> > Pardon me
> > How are you?
> > Excuse me
> > Bless you
> > May I?
> > Thank you
> > Goodbye
> If you know some that I've forgot,
> please stick them in your eye!

It's not enough just to learn the rules. As important as they are, it is more important to learn to love people—to really love and cherish and value people. That brings us to the second level of kindness.

The Level of Empathy

I love the word *empathy*. It means to feel *with* other people, to get in their shoes, to experience what they are experiencing. *Sympathy* means to feel sorry *for* someone; *empathy* is to feel sorry *with* someone.

In his syndicated column, D. L. Stewart spoke to the matter of empathy—that we sometimes become so preoccupied with our own little world that we forget to be empathetic, especially with those closest to us. He reflected on the preceding week:

After three gallons of cough syrup, a pound and a half of aspirin and a pile of Kleenex tall enough to endanger low flying aircraft, I have come to a conclusion: No one cares if you have a cold. I don't care what the TV commercials show. A wife will not get out of bed at 3 A.M to get you some nighttime cold medicine. Your children will not admire you for dragging yourself off to work in the morning with your nose running and your chest aching. Not even your best friend will listen to more than two symptoms. I know all this for a fact, because I had a cold last weekend.

It starts on Saturday morning, when I woke up with a sore throat, hacking cough and chills. I hack my way downstairs to the living room where two of my kids are sitting in front of the television. "Morning," I wheeze. They ignore me. There is a blanket on the floor next to my chair. I pull the blanket up under my chin and sit down, coughs wracking my body. The nine year old turns around and looks at me with concern. "Hey, Dad, could you please not cough so much? I can't hear the television." "Sorry," I wheeze. For an hour I sit there, doing my best to cough only during the commercials.

Finally, I wrap the blanket around my shoulders and go

into the kitchen for something to eat. I am in the middle of fixing a couple of poached Tylenols when the woman who promised to love, honor, and fill my vaporizer walks in. She sees me standing there with the blanket wrapped around my shoulders. "Don't tell me," she says. "They're putting on a Wild West Show at your office and you're going to be the squaw." "I hab a code," I said. "Well, try not to sneeze too much," she says, "That's the dog's favorite blanket."

That column is a light treatment of a very serious subject—how much we all need empathy, especially when we are hurting . . . and how often we fail to be empathetic with those closest to us. Sometimes we are not very tenderhearted.

One of the most beautiful expressions of kindness is at this level—empathy, the level of kindness that feels the pains, the hurts, the concerns, the frustrations, the agonies of others. The Scriptures tell us to rejoice with those who rejoice and weep with those who weep. Too often we turn that the other way around—we weep when others succeed and rejoice when others fail.

There is a story about a little girl who came home late from school and was questioned about her tardiness. She answered that her best friend's kitten had died, and she had stayed to help.

"How did you help?" her mother asked.

The little girl answered, "I helped her cry." That is the picture of empathy, a beautiful emblem of kindness, and it brings us to a still deeper level.

The Level of Christlike Kindness

Recall how the writer of Ephesians puts it: "Be kind to one another, be tenderhearted, forgiving one another, as God in Christ forgave you"—that is, imitate the spirit of kindness that was radiant in our Lord.

My father died as a result of an automobile accident when I was a young boy. It was on a Sunday afternoon. He had appendicitis and was being rushed to the hospital when the accident occurred. We walked the floor of the hospital and prayed in the chapel for several hours before we were sent home for the night.

Shortly after my brother and sister and I had fallen asleep, the hospital called to say that my father had died. Though I was only twelve, I have several vivid images of that tragic event. When the call came, the relatives who had gathered at our home decided to let us children sleep. They felt it was best that we get a good night's rest; they would tell us in the morning.

But they didn't know that I would get up early and go out to get the morning paper. When I opened it, there on the front page was the picture of our smashed-up car and the announcement that my dad had died in the wreck. Before anyone could tell me, I read it in the paper! As if it were yesterday, I remember sitting in the living room early that morning with the newspaper spread across my lap, and the relatives coming in and seeing me there and not knowing what to say. And I remember feeling sorry for them.

Another vivid image remains in my memory. That night at the funeral home, as we stood by my father's casket, scores of people came by—all kinds of people. Some were rich and some were poor; some were young and some were old; some were black, some were white, and some were Oriental. Some were professional people, some were laborers; some I knew quite well, some I had never seen before. But they all came. They came over and spoke to us to express their sympathy. Almost every one said the same thing: "Jim, your dad was kind to me." I determined then and there that the best tribute I could pay to my dad was to take up his torch of kindness. From that moment I have tried to be a kind person. I haven't always succeeded; but I have tried and I am still trying to let my father's kindness live on in me.

Please hold that in your mind for a moment, and remember with me what a kind person Jesus was. We give up on people, we write them off, we conclude there is no hope for them, we decide they are beyond redemption. But Jesus never did that. *He never relinquished his lovingkindness*. Even on the cross, he took care of his mother and forgave those who were putting him to death. To the very last, he was kind.

The best tribute we can pay him is to take up his torch of kindness, to love as he loved, care as he cared, forgive as he forgave, live as he lived, to the very last—in the spirit of kindness. The best tribute we can pay our Lord is to seize the moments of kindness and let his kindness live on in us.

12

The Moments of Creative Suffering

Genesis 50:15-21 When Joseph's brothers saw that their father was dead, they said, "It may be that Joseph will hate us and pay us back for all the evil which we did to him."

So they sent a message to Joseph, saying, "Your father gave this command before he died, 'Say to Joseph, Forgive, I pray you, the transgression of your brothers and their sin, because they did evil to you.' And now, we pray you, forgive the transgression of the servants of the God of your father." Joseph wept when they spoke to him. His brothers also came and fell down before him, and said, "Behold, we are your servants."

But Joseph said to them, "Fear not, for am I in the place of God? As for you, you meant evil against me; but God meant it for good, to bring it about that many people should be kept alive, as they are today. So do not fear; I will provide for you and your little ones." Thus he reassured them and comforted them.

A t one time or another, all of us will face trouble. It is universal and impartial, and not one of us is immune. There is no wall high enough to shut out trouble; there is no life, no matter how much it may be sheltered, that can escape; there is no trick, however clever, by which we can evade it. Sometime . . . somewhere—maybe even when we least expect it—things will go wrong! Trouble will rear its head, thrust its way into our lives, and confront and challenge every single one of us.

As Frank Sinatra used to sing, "Flying high in April, Shot down in May." So quickly life can cave in around us. We see this graphically in the Joseph story. One moment he was the fair-haired son of a well-to-do man, with bright hopes for a happy, secure, prosperous future; the next moment, his world had caved in around him; he became a slave in a strange, foreign land.

One thing has made Joseph live vividly in the minds of people over the years: His story is so true to life. We can relate to it. Of course, we can't be sold into slavery, but we all have things go wrong. In school, in business, in marriage, in health, in our hopes for our children, in our personal relationships—things can go wrong, things *do* go wrong. And when they do, we need to remember Joseph.

Joseph was one of the twelve sons of Jacob, his father's "favorite son." This favoritism, which Joseph enjoyed—and flaunted—didn't set well with Joseph's brothers. They were jealous, envious, resentful, bitter. In fact, Joseph's brothers became so hostile that they actually kidnapped him with the intention of murdering him. But when some slave traders came headed for Egypt, they sold him into slavery.

You recall the rest of the story: Joseph, through his faith in God and his unique ability to interpret dreams, eventually ended up as prime minister of Egypt and saved Egypt and his own family from famine. He then summed it up by saying to his brothers, "You meant evil against me; but God meant it for good" (15:20*b*).

The story of Joseph is a good one to remember when things go wrong; it underscores four basic questions most commonly raised when life caves in on us: Whose fault is this? How do we respond? How can this situation be redeemed? Where is God? Let's take a look at these questions.

Whose Fault Is This?

Why did this happen? What caused it? Who is at fault here? Where can we lay the blame? This is quite often our first response when things go wrong. We look for someone to blame.

This ploy is as old as the Garden of Eden. When things went wrong there, Adam pointed at Eve and Eve pointed at the serpent. Ultimately, they all pointed at God. When things go wrong we begin to look for someone to blame it on.

In the Joseph story, we could answer this question in several different ways. We could blame Joseph. He was partly at fault. He did fan the flames of his brothers' hostility with his swaggering bigheadedness. He was spoiled and childish. He did flaunt the fact that his father favored him. He did parade before them in his long flowing coat of many colors. He did tell on his brothers when he saw them doing something they shouldn't have been doing. He did arrogantly reveal his dreams in which his eleven brothers fell down to worship him.

But still, all this does not excuse his brothers for their cruel act of selling him into slavery and then deceiving their father into thinking Joseph was dead. Surely they were at fault. Then, too, it was the father's fault. If Jacob had shown more sense in dealing equally with his sons, Joseph probably never would have ended up as a slave in a foreign land.

But the truth is, it really doesn't matter who is at fault. The only real value derived from this kind of question is the hope that we can learn from our mistakes, grow from them, and do better next time. Too often when things go wrong, we evade facing the reality of the problem by spending too much time and effort in laying the blame on someone, and that really doesn't help. It was said about one fellow: "He met misfortune like a man—he blamed it on his wife!"

So when things go wrong, it is not nearly as important

to find who is at fault as it is to find the right way to respond to the problem.

How Do We Respond?

When things go wrong, we may or may not be responsible for the cause. But one thing is certain: We *are* responsible for the result, and the result depends on how we meet the situation, how we respond to trouble. There are two possibilities: We can respond either with *cowardice* or with *courage*. We can respond with weakness or strength, with bitterness or betterness.

Picture Joseph riding along in that slave caravan—scared, bewildered, panicky. How easy it would have been to choose the way of cowardice, to give in to self-pity, to quit on life. When things go wrong, many people do, indeed, choose that route. They blame God and die—maybe not physically, but emotionally, spiritually. They just give up, throw up their hands, toss in the towel.

But not so with Joseph. He grew up in that slave caravan. He had been spoiled, selfish, childish, but in that slave caravan he grew up and became a man. He chose the way of courage and trust in God. He didn't understand what was happening, but he kept on trying, and he trusted God to bring it out right.

When things go wrong, we must choose the way of courage. We must go on with life, doing the best we can, living one day at a time, trusting God to bring it out right. The psalmist did not say, "I will *meet* no evil"; he said, "I will *fear* no evil."

Psychologists tell us that we always have two conflicting desires: the temptation to shrink back and quit on life, to give in to cowardice and bitterness and self-pity; or the challenge to move forward, through struggle and effort and courage and perseverance, to a deeper dimension of life. And that is what Joseph did.

How Can This Situation Be Redeemed?

What could be a more Christian question than this for us, we who have as our major symbol a cross! That is what the cross is—a situation redeemed, a wrong turned right, a bad thing turned into a good thing, a defeat converted to a victory. In other words, be a "creative sufferer"; learn how to suffer creatively. Harry Emerson Fosdick said it this way:

> Quality of character never could have come from ease, comfort, and pleasantness alone. [Lincoln] did not simply endure his tragedies; he built character out of them. . . . Trouble and grief can add a new dimension to our life. No hardship, no hardihood; no fight, no fortitude; no suffering, no sympathy; no pain, no patience. . . . Don't waste sorrow, it is too precious. . . . Don't misunderstand me. I'm not singing a hymn of praise to trouble. We all alike dread it, but it is inevitably here to be dealt with one way or another. An old adage says, "The same fire that melts the butter hardens the egg." Some people end in defeat and collapse. . . . Others—thank God!—can say with Paul, "We triumph even in our troubles." (*Dear Mr. Brown* [New York: Harper & Brothers, 1961], pp. 182-83)

So many things went wrong for Joseph—betrayed by his own brothers, sold into slavery, thrown into prison, made the victim of a scorned woman—what a hopeless situation! But Joseph's ability to interpret dreams was made known to the Pharaoh, and the bad situation was redeemed.

Sometimes an oyster is invaded by a grain of sand. The sand irritates. The oyster tries to get rid of it. But when it cannot, it turns that same irritating grain of sand into a valuable pearl. That's redeeming the situation.

Thomas Edison had received a blow on his ear which made him deaf. But later, his deafness kept out distractions and enabled him to concentrate; the world has benefited greatly from that.

I read recently of a man whose eyes were seriously injured in an automobile accident. One eye could be saved, but the other would need to be removed.

The injured man instructed, "If you put in a glass eye, be sure to put in one with a twinkle!"

When things go wrong, the best question we can ask is this: How can this situation be redeemed?

Where Is God?

He is with us even closer than our hands and feet. And as we keep moving forward, living one day at a time, trusting in God and doing the best we can, he moves with us; he brings us through the valley. This is what Joseph referred to when he said to his brothers, "You meant evil against me; but God meant it for good." What had happened was bad, but God was with him through it all, every step of the way, and somehow in the miracle of his grace, God brought good out of those terrible events.

That is the good news of our faith. God is with us, and nothing, not even death, can separate us from him. "Lo, I am with you always"—this is God's most significant promise, and when we claim that promise, it changes our lives.

It is said that when Dean de Ovies was a little boy in England, he used to play in the cemetery at night. One night he accidentally fell into a newly dug grave so deep that he could not get out, no matter how he tried. Finally, in exhaustion, he sat down in the corner of the grave to wait till morning.

Suddenly he heard footsteps, then whistling, and he recognized the whistle of his friend Charlie. His first reaction was to cry out for help, but he decided to wait a while and see what would happen.

Sure enough, Charlie fell into the same grave. Dean de Ovies sat quietly in the dark corner as Charlie tried frantically to get out. After a while, de Ovies said loudly in a deep voice, "You can jump all you want to, Charlie, but you'll never get out of here!" *But Charlie did!* In a single bound, he went up and out of that grave as if he had wings!

There is a strong point here—the power of motivation. If one can be that strongly motivated by fear, why don't we turn the coin over? We can also be that strongly motivated by confidence!

"Lo, I am with you always"—this is the promise of God (Matt. 28:20b). And when trouble comes into our lives, we can claim that promise!

13

The Moments of Confidence

Matthew 27:20-26 Now the chief priests and the elders persuaded the people to ask for Barabbas and destroy Jesus. The governor again said to them, "Which of the two do you want me to release for you?" And they said, "Barabbas." Pilate said to them, "Then what shall I do with Jesus who is called Christ?" They all said, "Let him be crucified," And he said, "Why, what evil has he done?" But they shouted all the more, "Let him be crucified."

So when Pilate saw that he was gaining nothing, but rather that a riot was beginning, he took water and washed his hands before the crowd, saying, "I am innocent of this man's blood; see to it yourselves." And all the people answered, "His blood be on us and on our children!" Then he released for them Barabbas, and having scourged Jesus, delivered him to be crucified.

A year or so ago I was privileged to visit the Holy Land. One of the highlights of that trip was a visit to the courtyard in Jerusalem where Jesus was tried before Pontius Pilate. I was especially fascinated by one thing. Etched in the courtyard stones was a game called Basilinda, the first-century version of Monopoly or Trivial Pursuit, I suppose.

The game was played by the Roman guards, who weren't that happy to be in an occupied foreign country in the first place. And they weren't thrilled about being in Jerusalem during a religious festival that held little interest for them. They were there to keep order and to make sure no one tried to start an uprising of any kind. To pacify them and keep them entertained, they were allowed to play games in the courtyard.

This game was called Basilinda, which means "game of the king"; during the competition, a prisoner was selected to be dressed up like a king. The Roman soldiers thought it great sport to mock, taunt, and make fun of the prisoner, because they knew what was to come. For, you see, at the climax of a game, which took a week or so to complete, the winner had the right to decide the fate of the prisoner! He could do anything he wanted to the prisoner-king!

As our tour guide explained this, my mind darted back to that scene two thousand years ago when Jesus stood before Pontius Pilate as a prisoner-king. I found myself thinking afresh about the incredible poise and strength displayed by Jesus in that fearful situation. I realized as never before that one of the most impressive images of Holy Week is the *serenity of Jesus* in those difficult hours that led to the cross.

His *strength of character* is nothing short of amazing! His deep sense of peace, quiet confidence, inner calm, courage, serenity of spirit, power of purpose—call it what you will—that amazing quality of poise and composure stands out vividly! We see it even more dramatically as the Gospel writers set it alongside the nervous personality of Pontius Pilate.

Imagine with me that dramatic scene in which Jesus stands on trial before Pilate. What a contrast! How different these two men are! If we were to ask someone who knows nothing of the story to point out the strongest character, using our present-day standards, the person would point quickly to Pilate and confidently document that choice by underscoring the man's wealth, position, influential friends, power, connections, military might, authority, political clout, fame . . . and yet the choice would be wrong, wouldn't it? So very wrong! Because Jesus is the strong personality here, not Pilate.

But you see, in Jesus we discover a whole new, radically different understanding of *strength*. His approach startles us, it is so different: "He who would be great, or strong, let him be a servant!" Let him be a servant? Come on now! What on earth can Jesus mean? "Strong, confident people aren't servants; they *have* servants!" we protest. What is Jesus trying to do here— upset our whole scale of values? *Yes!* That is precisely what he is trying to do—to give us a whole new set of values, a new perspective, a new measuring stick, a new standard for defining real strength.

Look at that trial scene again in light of this. Who has the strength here? Who has the power? Who is courageous?

Not Pilate. He has the outer circumstances, but not the inner stability. Outwardly, he is in control, but inside he is a wreck. It's obvious, isn't it? Jesus is the strong one. In fact, his inner strength, his poise, his serenity completely baffle Pilate.

Look at Pilate: He is confused, weak. He can't make up his mind. In a dither, he runs from one group to the other, asking questions here and there. He tries to pass the buck to Herod. Pilate knows Jesus is innocent, but he does not have the strength of character to stand firm for what is right. This is the picture of a man running scared. Outwardly, he has it all—power, wealth, position, fame; but inwardly, where it really counts, he is scared to death, "nervous as a long-tailed cat in a room full of rocking chairs!"

Finally he tries to straddle the fence. Like a nervous politician, he gives the people what they want. He turns Jesus over to them for execution, but just in case someone else might see it differently, he washes his hands, acts as if he is not really involved.

Is that strength of character? Is that courage? Is that

peace of mind, serenity of spirit? Are fright, confusion, and weakness signs of strength? Surely not!

But look at Jesus! He stands there poised, confident, unafraid. He is facing ridicule, pain, and death, but his strength never wavers! Just think of it—an unfair trial for an innocent man; lies, plotting, conniving, scheming; bribed witnesses, political intrigue, jealousy, hostility, hatred; a mob scene; a kangaroo court. And in the face of it all, Jesus stands tall. They betray him, deny him, taunt him, beat him, curse him, spit upon him, nail him to a cross, and he says, "Father, forgive them, they know not what they do!"

Now, that is strength of character! That is inner peace, serenity. Real serenity comes not from outer circumstances or power or position or possessions. It comes from inner stability, and in that respect, Jesus was the most serene person who ever lived. But where did that strength come from? What produced that amazing poise and peace and confidence, that strong moral fiber? Simply this: He knew who he was; he knew where he was going; he knew Who was with him. When we know those things, it sets us free; it gives us an amazing sense of peace and incredible strength of character. Let's take a quick look at those three things.

He Knew Who He Was.

Jesus was God's Son, who had come to show us that we are God's children. You see, we don't have to run scared. We can be confident! That attitude is a by-product of Christian faith.

Someone once asked the great preacher Phillips Brooks why he was so confident and optimistic about life. He answered, "Because I am a Christian!" So simple and yet so profound! We can be confident because God loves us. He claims us as his children. He will ultimately win the victory, and he wants to share that victory with us.

When you know that you are God's child, that he is watching over you, that nothing, not even death, can separate you from his watchful care—O what strength comes from that!

One Saturday morning some years ago, I was running errands. Our son, Jeff, about five years old at the time, was with me. When we pulled into a service station the attendant recognized me, and as we talked, he called me Reverend.

When we left, Jeff said, "Dad, you have lots of names."

"What do you mean?" I asked.

He explained. "Well, some people call you Reverend, some call you Brother, some call you Pastor, and most call you Jim."

"Well, I suppose that's right," I replied. Then I asked, "By the way, which name do you like best?"

I'll never forget his answer: "I guess they are all O.K., but best of all, I like Daddy!"

Over the years, God has been given many names: Creator, First Cause, Unmoved Mover, Supreme Being, Ultimate Reality, Cosmic Force. I guess all these names are O.K., but it is significant to note that when Jesus said the best thing he could think of to say about God, he used the image of a loving parent who cares for and watches over his children.

Jesus knew who he was. He knew he was God's child, and he knew his Father could be trusted; when we believe that, it gives us courage and confidence and strength of character.

He Knew Where He Was Going.

Jesus had a sense of purpose, and as a result, he had tremendous power. He had set his face toward Jerusalem. He had made up his mind to strike a blow for justice, come what may.

When you make up your mind, when you have a purpose, when you set your face, when you know where you are going, you are given great strength. Jesus knew who he was and he knew where he was going.

He Knew Who Was with Him.

The great Old Testament scholar Martin Buber said something toward the end of his life that touched me greatly. He was commenting on that wonderful scene in the book of Exodus when Moses asked God, "What is your name?" and God answered, "I am who I am."

After studying the Hebrew text for many years, Martin Buber had come to the conclusion that we have mistranslated that verse. Instead of being translated "I am who I am," Buber believed it should read: "I Shall Be There!" Isn't that beautiful? The name of God is I Shall Be There!

When we face the pharaohs of life, the name of God is I Shall Be There. When we are frightened or lonely or depressed, the name of God is I Shall be There. When we face sickness, heartache, or even death, the name of God is I Shall Be There. When we must go to a cross, the name of God is I Shall Be There. When we are laid out in tombs, the name of God is I Shall Be There. And when Easter morning comes, the name of God is I Shall Be There.

Jesus knew that. That's why he was so strong. He knew who he was. He knew where he was going. And he knew Who was with him. Do we?

14

The Moments of Childlikeness

Mark 10:13-16 And they were bringing children to him, that he might touch them; and the disciples rebuked them. But when Jesus saw it he was indignant, and said to them, "Let the children come to me, do not hinder them; for to such belongs the kingdom of God. Truly, I say to you, whoever does not receive the kingdom of God like a child shall not enter it." And he took them in his arms and blessed them, laying his hands upon them.

S ome time ago a successful young businessman came to see me. He was the epitome of the yuppie, the young urban professional, the outstanding junior executive who well may be president of a company someday. He was bright, handsome, personable, talented, with a lovely wife and four beautiful children. I almost envied him and his bright prospects for the future. But as we talked, I realized he had a problem. He was deeply troubled. And he wanted to talk about it.

He blurted it out: "I'm miserable. There is something missing in my life. I have everything I have ever dreamed of having, but something is wrong. I'm doing well financially. I'm successful in my work. I'm respected in the community. But I feel empty. I'm on edge all the time, irritable and tense. My marriage is on the rocks, and I'm not enjoying the children as I should. I feel all panicky inside. I need help!"

He paused a moment, looked down at the floor, then continued, "I know what my problem is. I have lost the quality of childlikeness. The child-ego state has vanished from my personality. Over the years, I have become too sophisticated, too businesslike, cold and calculating. I never relax, I never let my hair down, I never have fun. I'm too busy playing the success game, polishing my image. I have become cynical and skeptical. I don't trust anyone anymore. I have given so much of myself, for so long, to being the tough-minded, aggressive, success-at-any-cost businessman that I have lost the quality of childlikeness. There's no little boy in me anymore . . . and I'm the loser for that!"

Well, what do you think? Was the young executive seeing it clearly? Was he on target? Was he saying something we all need to hear? I have to be honest—I do think he is right—that we need to become more childlike. The pressures of our society do tend to make us cold and calculating and image-conscious. Of course, we want to be mature, but the quality of childlikeness is a part of that maturity, and it's an essential ingredient in happiness and joy and enthusiasm . . . and in Christian discipleship.

We see it in Mark 10. Jesus has come to the region of Judea, and great crowds are coming to see him and hear him teach. Jesus gets into heavy discussion with the Pharisees on some weighty matters of ethics. And then come the little children. At this point, the disciples (perhaps caught up in their own self-importance as followers of the great teacher) see the children as a nuisance, an annoyance, a disturbance, so they begin to direct traffic. "Get back there, you kids! Get those children out of here! This is serious business! We don't have time for this! We are doing big things here! Don't bother the master! Get back and keep quiet. He doesn't have time for children!"

Now, can't you just picture the disciples striding around boldly, acting big, pompously barking out orders? They remind me of Barney Fife on the old Andy Griffith television show, strutting proudly through the streets of Mayberry, directing traffic, caught up in his own self-importance, polishing his image, taking himself too seriously—his chest stuck way out, his badge shining— reminding everybody that he is the law, the deputy sheriff of Mayberry.

The disciples here in Mark 10 remind me of Mr. Neilson. He was the head usher in his church, and he was a good usher until he went to Usher School. The church paid his way to the week-long school—and did that church ever live to regret it! When he returned, he was so overtrained that his ushering took on gigantic proportions. He became the main event at worship services. He directed people in a fashion similar to a combination of enthusiastic traffic cop, Leonard Bernstein conducting the New York Philharmonic, and ringmaster of the Barnum and Bailey circus. Mr. Neilson gave so much effort to shushing the children and youth that they began to refer to him as the Head Husher!

I am also reminded of a Pee Wee Football game I attended some years ago. The sponsor of the pep squad for one of the teams had her fifth-grade girls sitting prim and proper, with neat uniforms and white gloves, doing their cheers very systematically. I was sitting just behind them.

All went well until their team scored a touchdown. Then the little girls came unglued. They jumped up and down and cheered and squealed and hugged one another, doing magnificent high-fives. This infuriated the sponsor! Red-faced, she screamed at them to sit down, straighten up their rows, be more proper.

She said harshly, "I'm ashamed of all of you. When I was your age I was in a pep squad, and I never acted like that!"

Then I heard one of the little girls mutter, "She was never our age!"

Somehow over the years the quality of childlikeness had become lost. You could see her problem written strongly in the worried look always on her face.

In similar fashion, the disciples rebuked the children that day in Judea. But when Jesus saw what they were doing he was displeased: "No! No! Let the children come to me! Remember this—whoever does not receive the kingdom of God like a little child shall not enter it!"

Jesus' reference here obviously is not to child*ish*ness, but to child*like*ness. He probably was drawing attention to the qualities of genuineness, receptivity, dependence, trust, openness, affection, curiosity, energy, enthusiasm, joy, and wonder.

All these are characteristic of children, and they also are characteristic of the Christian life-style. Elton Trueblood said it well in "The Heart of a Child":

> We tend to glorify adulthood and wisdom and worldly prudence, but the Gospel reverses all this. The Gospel says that the inescapable condition of entrance into the divine fellowship is that we turn and become as a little child, tender and full of wonder and unspoiled by the hard skepticism on which we so often pride ourselves. God has sent children into the world, not only to replenish it, but to serve also as sacred reminders of something ineffably precious which we are always in danger of losing. The sacrament of childhood is thus a continuing education.

A few years ago, someone sent me a fascinating book, *Children's Letters to God* by Eric Marshall and Stuart Hample. You may have seen it. It's just what the title says, a collection of "authentic letters" written to God. They are moving, poignant, humorous—touching messages from the minds of children:

SOME PRAYER REQUESTS:

"Dear God, My dad can never get a fire started in the grill. Could you please make a 'burning bush' in our yard? Sherry."

"Dear God, I would like all the bad things to stop. Debbie."

"Dear God, My father is mean sometimes. Please get him not to be. But, please God, don't hurt him. Sincerely, Martin."

SUGGESTIONS:

"Dear God, The people in the next apartment fight real loud all the time. You should only let very good friends get married. Nan."

GENUINE OFFERS:

"Dear God, I made 25¢ selling lemonade. I will give you some of it Sunday. Chris."

"Dear God, I am sending you a penny to give to a kid poorer than me. Love, Donna."

"Dear God, A lot of people say bad things with your name in it, but I never do. Helen."

EARNEST INQUIRIES:

"Dear God, Where did everybody come from? I hope you explain it better than my father. Ward."

"Dear God, Did you mean for giraffes to look like that —or was it an accident? Norman."

"Dear God, Can you marry food? Martha."

PRAISE:

"Dear God, I didn't think orange went very good with purple until I saw the sunset you made last Tuesday. That was cool. Eugene."

"Dear God, Did you think up hugging? That is a good thing! Brenda."

"Dear God, Count me in. Your friend, Herbie."

Aren't those beautiful? Here in these wonderful letters we see some of the special ingredients of childlikeness— the sense of wonder and curiosity, the attitude of dependence and trust, the spirit of open-mindedness and humility, enthusiasm and love. How tragic if we become so sophisticated and proud, so pompous and calculating, that we lose the "little child" in us!

Jesus felt this strongly. He loved children. He liked the quality of childlikeness; he called it the key to entering the Kingdom.

I would like to share with you some more messages from the minds of children—"mistakes" that actually preach the gospel. Harry Emerson Fosdick called them "happy mistranslations"—things children mislearned and accidentally came up with something just as good, if not better.

> *"Our Father who art in New Haven,*
> *How did you know my name?"*

Here in this childlike mistranslation, a little girl from New Haven captured, in her own way, one of the basic messages of the Sermon on the Mount—that God is our loving Father, who is with us wherever we are, in every circumstance of life; that he knows our names and he cares for us.

This childlike faith and trust is expressed wonderfully in these lines from an old spiritual:

> What you gonna do when it comes on night?
>   Trust in God and hold on tight.
> What you gonna do when your strength gives way?
>   Say "Howdy, Lord, it's judgment day!"

Isn't that just another way of saying, "Our Father who art in New Haven—or Houston—how did you know my name?"

> *"The Lord is my shepherd,*
>   *that's all that I want!"*

When some little boy mislearned the first part of the Twenty-third Psalm, he said it all. Isn't that beautiful? That's the good news of our faith—if we have God with us, that's all we need.

It reminds me of Dietrich Bonhoeffer's prayer in the prison camp: "Lord, whatever this day may bring, Thy name be praised!" Can we say that? Do we have the quality of childlikeness that would enable us to trust God so completely? That prayer is another way of saying: "The Lord is my shepherd, that's all that I want!"

By the way, someone once said something very interesting about Bonhoeffer: "He was a giant before men because he was a child before God!" Isn't that a wonderful tribute?

> *"Forgive us our trash baskets,*
> *as we forgive those who trash basket against us."*

A little girl who misunderstood the words of the Lord's Prayer came up with that.

Some years ago when Henry Kissinger was Secretary of

State, there was a story about an excited and overly ambitious young reporter who went through Kissinger's garbage looking for a story. It seems you can learn a lot about people by looking through their trash baskets.

What would our trash baskets reveal about us? Maybe we all need to pray, along with that child, "Forgive us our trash baskets!"

"If I should wake before I die!"

Here a little boy mixed up the familiar bedtime prayer. As Charlie Brown might put it, "Why, the theological implications are staggering!"

The fact is that many of us do need to wake up. We have dozed off into indifference. Let me point out something very interesting in the Scripture Mark 10. Remember how the incident develops:

- The children come.
- The disciples try to block them.
- Jesus sees what is happening and is displeased.
- He calls for the children to come to him.
- He brings them into the inner circle.
- He takes them into his arms and blesses them.
- He says that in order to get into the kingdom of God, we should be like little children.

Then notice this: Immediately after the episode with the children, Mark records the story of the rich young ruler who has everything exalted by the adult world—wealth, youth, power, authority, prestige, clout—and yet something is missing. There is an emptiness, a void, a hunger, an aching for something more. So he comes to Jesus in search of real life. But when Jesus lays down the cost of discipleship, the rich young ruler turns away sorrowfully. Why? Because he is too sophisticated, too proud, too success-oriented, too image-conscious. "What would people say? After all, I'm a man of position," he reasons.

You see, he could not follow Christ because he could not become like a little child. He was too set in his ways, too cynical, too skeptical, too businesslike, cold, and calculating. He couldn't quite believe that God knew his name. He couldn't quite believe that God's shepherding was all he needed. He couldn't walk away from his trash baskets. He couldn't wake up to the new treasure Jesus was offering.

Now, what about us. Couldn't we use a little childlikeness? Let me conclude with a poem by Andrew Gillies, "Two Prayers."

> Last night my little boy confessed to me
> Some childish wrong;
> And kneeling at my knee,
> He prayed with tears—
> "Dear God, make me a man
> Like Daddy—wise and strong;
> I know you can."
>
> Then while he slept
> I knelt beside his bed,
> Confessed my sins,
> And prayed with low-bowed head—
> "O God, make me a child
> Like my child here—
> Pure, guileless,
> Trusting Thee with faith sincere."

15

The Right Words for the Moment

John 1:1-18 In the beginning was the Word, and the Word was with God, and the Word was God. He was in the beginning with God; all things were made through him, and without him was not anything made that was made. In him was life, and the life was the light of men. The light shines in the darkness, and the darkness has not overcome it.

There was a man sent from God, whose name was John. He came for testimony, to bear witness to the light, that all might believe through him. He was not the light, but came to bear witness to the light.

The true light that enlightens every man was coming into the world. He was in the world, and the world was made through him, yet the world knew him not. He came to his own home, and his own people received him not. But to all who received him, who believed in his name, he gave power to become children of God; who were born, not of blood nor of the will of the flesh nor of the will of man, but of God.

And the Word became flesh and dwelt among us, full of grace and truth; we have beheld his glory, glory as of the only Son from the Father. (John bore witness to him, and cried, "This was he of whom I said, 'He who comes after me ranks before me, for he was before me.' ")

And from his fulness have we all received, grace upon grace. For the law was given through Moses; grace and truth came through Jesus Christ. No one has ever seen God; the only Son, who is in the bosom of the Father, he has made him known.

L earning the right words—how important that is! What we say (and how we say it) reveals a lot about who we are and what we believe.

A friendly postman struck up a conversation with a four-year-old boy about his baby sister: "Can she talk?"

"No," the little boy answered. "She has her teeth, but her words haven't come in yet!"

That is an important part of the growing-up process— getting the words in . . . getting the *right* words in.

- The right words can bring peace. The wrong words can cause war and destruction.
- The right words can bring harmony. The wrong words can cause discord and suspicion.
- The right words can bring healing. The wrong words can cause pain and sickness.
- The right words can produce love. The wrong words can spread hatred and hostility.

Words are so important, so powerful, so influential. A word can excite or a word can depress. A word can make us glad or sad or mad. Words can inspire and lift our spirits or depress and deflate our souls. Words can motivate and encourage or they can crush and kill. Words can compel us to stand firm for what is right and good and true, or they can destroy hope, blast reputations, take the wind out of our sails. Words can offer a beautiful prayer, preach a powerful sermon; or they can incite a riot, tell a dirty joke. It's so important to learn the right words, the words of life—words that are creative, not destructive. Isn't that what we are about in the church and in our homes? We are trying to learn the right words.

Some months ago we were considering hiring a new secretary for our church staff. One woman impressed us greatly. There was something extra-special about her. We realized what it was when we visited with people who knew her and people who had worked with her. They all said, "She always knows just the right thing to say. In any situation, she has the remarkable ability to come up with the right words!" We hired her immediately!

And that is one of the highest compliments we can pay. It is a mark of maturity to know the right words. That's what we all are trying to learn—the ability to use the right words.

I guess it always has been that way. Hitler almost brought the world to its knees with his oratory, and he might have succeeded, had it not been for the inspired and eloquent words of Winston Churchill. In *Still the Trumpet Sounds*, J. Wallace Hamilton reported a speech made by Ann Blyth some time ago. Most of the fifteen hundred Hollywood personages who heard the talk asked for a copy:

> In the beginning was the word . . . And since then a billion, million words have been spoken. Soft words, hard words, cold words, warm words. There are words that sing and jump and skip and dance—gay words: little girl words. And words with fun in their eyes and things in their pockets and their hair mussed: little boy words. There are young words. And wise old words with a glint in their eye. There are words wide-eyed with wonder, warm, cuddly words, soft as a baby's feet. And steel words . . . stinging . . . cruel blades of words—and sweet words that press their cheek against yours. . . . Words are everything. . . . In a world at the mercy of the word of God, man is at the mercy of words. ([Old Tappan, N.J.: Fleming H. Revell, 1970], p. 155)

Communication—what a miracle! The transmission of ideas through words—no mystery is greater than that. "In the beginning was the Word." Everything—understanding, friendship, communication with other people and with God—it all begins with a word. We do not live by bread alone. We live by words. All the things that are done in the world—good or bad—are done through words.

Recently I heard about a wealthy Texan who was highly cultured and also owned lots of land, cattle, and oil. She decided to take her son, Reginald, into Houston to do some shopping. As they walked down the street they saw two cowboys.

Reginald said, "Lookee yonder, Momma, at them thar bowlegged cowboys!"

Reginald's mother, aghast at this manner of speaking, realized he had been spending too much time with the ranch hands, so she sent him away to college. The next summer they came back into Houston to shop, and as luck would have it, they saw two more bowlegged cowboys.

This time Reginald said, "Hark! What manner of men are these / who wear their legs in parentheses!" The pendulum had swung too far, but at least his spirit was right. He was trying to learn the right words.

Let's look now at some "life-words," words we need to cultivate in the home and in the church.

Words of Kindness

It is not necessary to be rude or harsh or hateful or hostile. We can be kind. We can speak words of kindness. As I said before, one of the most important signs of Christian faith is kindness. In *The Little Locksmith*, Katherine Hathaway describes Catharine Huntington, whom she had met at Radcliffe College:

> This was her talent to discern in an obscure person something rare and important and to make other people see it too—above all, to make the person in question feel it and be it.
>
> She could hold an utterly unprepossessing person up in a certain light, like a collector showing a rare piece, and the person, in her hands, would suddenly receive a value and importance which made the people who watched the transformation wonder how they could have been so blind as never to have seen it before. ([Salem, N.H.: Ayer Co. Publications, 1943], pp. 178-79)

Words of kindness are words of life for those who hear
them and for those who speak them. They are words of
life, words we are trying to teach our children—words we
ourselves are, indeed, trying to learn.

Words of Appreciation

It is not necessary to be thoughtless. We do not need to
take things or people for granted. We can be grateful. We
can make the sounds of thanksgiving. We can learn the
words of appreciation.

People are hungry for appreciation. How long has it
been since you young people expressed appreciation to
your parents? It may shock them a little, but why not give
it a try?

Parents, do you ever tell your children how proud you
are of them, how grateful you are for them? They would
like to hear it. As a matter of fact, they *need* to hear it.

You who are married, how long has it been since you
expressed your appreciation to your wife or husband?

We can learn the words of appreciation by continually
expressing thanks for specific things until it becomes a
habit. Why not try it today? But let me warn you—it
could change your life!

Parents, whether we realize it or not, we are teaching
our children either gratitude or ingratitude. We are
teaching them by the way we act and speak and treat them
and other people . . . and each other. An old fairy tale
underscores this powerfully:

> Once upon a time, there was a little old man. His eyes
> blinked and his hands trembled; when he ate, he clattered
> the silverware, often missed his mouth with the spoon, and
> dribbled his food on the tablecloth.
>   Now, he lived with his married son, having nowhere else
> to live, and his son's wife did not approve of such sloppy
> table manners.

So she and her husband took the old man gently but firmly and led him to the corner of the fireplace. There they sat him on a stool and gave him his food in a bowl. From then on he always ate in the corner, blinking at the table with wistful eyes.

One day his hands trembled more than usual and his bowl fell and broke on the floor.

"If you are a pig," said the daughter-in-law, "you must eat out of a trough." So they made him a little wooden trough and thereafter he ate his meals from that.

Now, these people had a four-year-old son whom they loved deeply. One evening they noticed the young boy playing with some pieces of wood, and his father asked what he was doing.

"I'm making a trough," he said, smiling up for approval, "to feed you and Momma out of when I get big."

The man and his wife looked at each other. Then they cried a little. Then they went to the corner, took the little old man by the arm, and led him back to the table. They sat him in a comfortable chair and gave him his food on a plate, and from then on, nobody ever scolded when he clattered his silverware or spilled his food or broke things.

Old fairy tales can be really "grimm"! But maybe that's the way we need to hear things sometimes, to remind us that our children learn from watching us. Be honest now! What are you teaching your children about gratitude? Or about ingratitude? Are you teaching them words of kindness? Are you teaching them words of appreciation?

Words of Love

Jesus is the measuring stick for the words of love:

- He spoke words of *tenderness:* "Come to me, all who labor and are heavy laden, and I will give you rest (Matt. 11:28).

- He spoke words of *peace:* "Peace I leave with you; my peace I give to you" (John 14:27).
- He spoke words of *hope:* "In my Father's house are many rooms" (John 14:2).
- He spoke words of *forgiveness:* "Father, forgive them" (Luke 32:34).
- He spoke words of *love:* "A new commandment I give to you, that you love one another; even as I have loved you . . . By this all men will know that you are my disciples" (John 13:34, 35).

Jesus constructively criticized the wrong and strongly defended the right, but always there was love and mercy. And when he spoke, people heard and saw God.

This is our calling: to so speak that our words reflect kindness, appreciation, and love; to so speak that people can hear, through our feeble words, the eternal Word of God; to so speak that our words fill the air—not with the sounds of hate or hostility, not with the sounds of temper or cruelty, not with the sounds of jealousy or vengeance or self-pity, but with the words of life—the words of *love!*